MIDDLE SCHOOL EDITION

Differentiating Instruction With Menus

Math

Laurie E. Westphal

PRUFROCK PRESS INC.

WACO, TEXAS

Prufrock Press Inc.
P.O. Box 8813
Waco, TX 76714-8813
Phone: (800) 998-2208
Fax: (800) 240-0333
http://www.prufrock.com

Differentiating Instruction With Menus

Math

For Cheryl, whom I met in Mr. Murray's geometry
class at RHS. Thank goodness you had a W name!
You have always supported my dreams
and for that I am grateful.

CONTENTS

Part 1
All About Choice and Menus

CHAPTER 1

Choice

"**O**h my gosh! THAAAAANK YOU!" exclaimed one of my students as he fell to his knees dramatically in the middle of my classroom. I had just handed out a list menu on the periodic table and told my class they would be able to choose how they wanted to learn the material.

Why Is Choice Important to Middle School Students?

" . . . Almost every kid in middle school wants freedom of his or her choice of what they want to work on. They just do."

—Eighth-grade math student

First, we have to consider who (or what) our middle school students personify. During these years, adolescents struggle to determine who they are and how they fit into the world around them. They constantly try new ideas (the hydrogen peroxide in the hair sounded like a good idea at the time), new experiences (if you sit on the second-floor roof of your home one more time, I will tell your parents!), and constant flux of personali-

3

ties (preppy one day, dark nails and lipstick the next) in order to obtain "zen" and find themselves. During this process, which can take from a few months to a few years depending on the child, academics are not always at the forefront of his mind unless the student has chosen that as part of his identity. Knowing this, instruction and higher level products have to engage the individuals these students are trying to become.

> ## "I like choice because I get to make decisions on my own. For myself!"
> *—Seventh-grade science student*

Ask adults whether they would prefer to choose what to do or be told what to do, and of course, they are going to say they would prefer to have a choice. Students have the same feelings, especially middle school students. Academics usually have been pushed back in priority as they seek to find themselves, so implementing choice as a way to engage these students has many explicit benefits once it has been developed as the center of high-level thinking.

> ## "I like being able to choose, because I can pick what I am good at and avoid my weaknesses."
> *—Eighth-grade language arts student*

One benefit of choice is its ability to meet the needs of so many different students and their learning styles. The Dunedin College of Education (Keen, 2001) conducted a research study on the preferred learning styles of 250 gifted students. Students were asked to rank different learning options. Of the 13 different options described to the students, only one option did not receive at least one negative response, and that was the option of having a choice. Although all students have different learning styles and preferences, choice is the one option that can meet everyone's needs. Unlike elementary students, middle school students have been engaged in the learning process long enough that they usually can recognize their own strengths and weaknesses, as well their learning styles. By allowing choice, students are able to choose what best fits their learning styles and educational needs.

> ". . . I am different in the way I do stuff. I like to build stuff with my hands more than other things."
> —*Sixth-grade student*

Another benefit of choice is a greater sense of independence for the students. What a powerful feeling! Students will be designing and creating a product based on what they envision, rather than what their teacher envisions. When students would enter my middle school classroom, they often had been trained by previous teachers to produce exactly what the teacher wanted, not what the students thought would be best. Teaching my students that what they envision could be correct (and wonderful) was a struggle. "Is this what you want? or "Is this right?" were popular questions as we started the school year. Allowing students to have choices in the products they create to show their learning helps create independence at an early age.

> "It [choice] puts me in a good mood to participate!"
> —*Seventh-grade student*

Strengthened student focus on the required content is a third benefit. Middle school students already have begun to transition from an academic focus to more of a social one. Choice is a way to help bring their focus back to the academic aspect of school. When students have choices in the activities they wish to complete, they are more focused on the learning that leads to their choice product. Students become excited when they learn information that can help them develop a product they would like to create. Students will pay close attention to instruction and have an immediate application for the knowledge being presented in class. Also, if students are focused, they are less likely to be off task during instruction.

Many a great educator has referred to the idea that the best learning takes place when the students have a desire to learn. Some middle school students still have a desire to learn anything that is new to them, but many others do not want to learn anything unless it is of interest to them. By incorporating different activities from which to choose, students stretch beyond what they already know, and teachers create a void that needs to be filled. This void leads to a desire to learn.

How Can Teachers Provide Choices?

"The GT students seem to get more involved in assignments when they have choice. They have so many creative ideas and the menus give them the opportunity to use them."

—*Social studies teacher*

When people go to a restaurant, the common goal is to find something on the menu to satisfy their hunger. Students come into our classrooms having a hunger as well—a hunger for learning. Choice menus are a way of allowing our students to choose how they would like to satisfy that hunger. At the very least, a menu is a list of choices that students use to choose an activity (or activities) they would like to complete to show what they have learned. At best, it is a complex system in which students earn points by making choices from different areas of study. All menus also should incorporate a free-choice option for those "picky eaters" who would like to place a special order to satisfy their learning hunger.

Tic-Tac-Toe Menu

"They [Tic-Tac-Toe Menus] can be a real pain. A lot of times I only liked two of the choices and had to do the last one. Usually I got stuck with a play or presentation."

—*Sixth-grade math student (asked to step out of her comfort zone based on the tic-tac-toe design)*

Description

The Tic-Tac-Toe menu (see Figure 1.1) is a basic menu with a total of eight predetermined choices and one free choice for students. All choices are created at the same level of Bloom's Revised taxonomy (Anderson et al., 2001). All carry the same weight for grading and have similar expectations for completion time and effort.

Benefits

Flexibility. This menu can cover one topic in depth, or three different objectives. When this menu covers just one objective, students have the option of completing three products in a tic-tac-toe pattern, or simply picking three from the menu. When it covers three objectives, students will need to complete a tic-tac-toe pattern (one in each column or row) to be sure they have completed one activity from each objective.

Friendly Design. Students quickly understand how to use this menu.

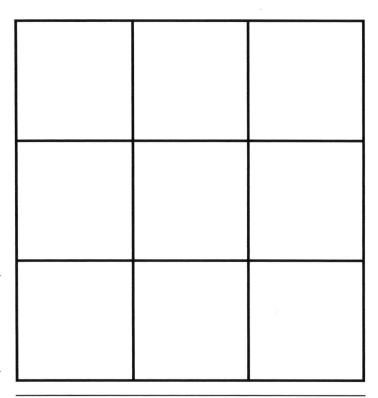

Figure 1.1. Tic-tac-toe menu.

Weighting. All products are equally weighted, so recording grades and maintaining paperwork is easily accomplished with this menu.

Limitations

Few Topics. These menus only cover one or three topics.

Short Time Period. They are intended for shorter periods of time, between 1–3 weeks.

Student Compromise. Although this menu does allow choice, a student will sometimes have to compromise and complete an activity he or she would not have chosen because it completes his or her tic-tac-toe. (This is not always bad, though!)

Time Considerations

These menus usually are intended for shorter amounts of completion time—at the most, they should take 3 weeks. If it focuses on one topic in-depth, the menu could be completed in one week.

List Menu

"I like that you can add up the points to be over 100, so even if you make some small mistakes, your grade could still be a 100."

—*Seventh-grade student*

Description

The List Menu (see Figure 1.2), or Challenge List, is a more complex menu than the Tic-Tac-Toe Menu, with a total of at least 10 predetermined choices, each with its own point value, and at least one free choice for students. Choices are simply listed with assigned points based on the levels of Bloom's Revised taxonomy. The choices carry different weights and have different expectations for completion time and effort. A point criterion is set forth that equals 100%, and students choose how they wish to attain that point goal.

Benefits

Responsibility. Students have complete control over their grades. They really like the idea that they can guarantee their grade if they complete their required work. If they lose points on one of the chosen assignments, they can complete another to be sure they have met their goal points.

Concept Reinforcement. This menu also allows for an in-depth study of material; however, with the different levels of Bloom's Revised taxonomy being represented, students who are still learning the concepts can choose

Figure 1.2. List menu.

some of the lower level point value projects to reinforce the basics before jumping into the higher level activities.

Limitations

Few Topics. This menu is best used for one topic in depth, although it can be used for up to three different topics.

Cannot Guarantee Objectives. If it is used for three topics, it is possible for a student to not have to complete an activity for each objective, depending on the choices he or she makes.

Preparation. Teachers need to have all materials ready at the beginning of the unit for students to be able to choose any of the activities on the list, which requires advanced planning.

Time Considerations

These menus usually are intended for shorter amounts of completion time—at the most, 2 weeks.

2–5–8 or 20-50-80 Menu

> "My least favorite menu is 2-5-8. You can't just do the easy ones. If you pick a 2, then you gotta do an 8, or you have to do 2 5s. I don't think you should do any more of these. No matter what you had to do one of hard ones."
>
> —Seventh-grade student

Description

A 2-5-8 Menu (see Figure 1.3), or 20-50-80 Menu, has two variations: one in which the activities are worth 2, 5, or 8 points, and one in which the activities are worth 20, 50, or 80. The 20, 50, and 80 version often is easier to grade with a rubric based on 5s (like the one included in this book). Both are variations on a List Menu, with a total of at least eight predetermined choices: at least two choices with a point value

Figure 1.3. 2-5-8 menu.

of 2 (20), at least four choices with a point value of 5 (50), and at least two choices with a point value of 8 (80). Choices are assigned these points based on the levels of Bloom's Revised taxonomy. Choices with a point value of two represent the *remember* and *understand* levels, choices with a point value of five represent the *apply* and *analyze* levels, and choices with a point value of eight represent the *evaluate* and *create* levels. All levels of choices carry different weights and have different expectations for completion time and effort. Students are expected to earn 10 (100) points for a 100%. Students choose what combination they would like to use to attain that point goal.

Benefits

Responsibility. With this menu, students still have complete control over their grades.

Guaranteed Activity. This menu's design also is set up in such a way that students must complete at least one activity at a higher level of Bloom's Revised taxonomy in order to reach their point goal.

Limitations

One Topic. Although it can be used for more than one topic, this menu works best with in-depth study of one topic.

No Free Choice. By nature, it also does not allow students to propose their own free choice, because point values need to be assigned based on Bloom's Revised taxonomy.

Higher Level Thinking. Students will complete only one activity at a higher level of thinking.

Time Considerations

These menus are usually intended for a shorter amount of completion time—at the most, one week.

Baseball Menu

"There were so many choices and most of them were fun activities!"

−Sixth-grade student

Description

This menu (see Figure 1.4) is a baseball-based variation on the List Menu, with a total of at least 20 predetermined choices: Choices are given values as singles, doubles, triples, or home runs based on Bloom's Revised taxonomy. Singles represent the *remember* and *understand* levels; doubles, the *apply* and *analyze* levels; triples, the *evaluate* level; and home runs, the *create* level. All levels of choices carry different weights and have different expectations for completion time and effort. Students are expected to earn a certain number of runs (around all four bases) for a 100%. Students choose what combination they would like to use to attain that number of runs.

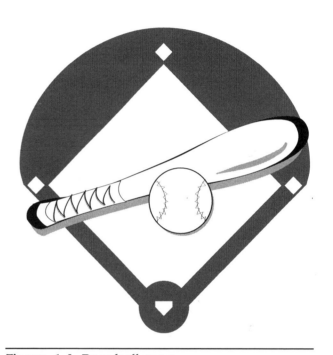

Figure 1.4. Baseball menu.

Benefits

Responsibility. With this menu, students still have complete control over their own grades.

Flexibility. This menu allows for many choices at each level. Students should have no trouble finding something that catches their interest.

Theme. This menu has a fun theme that students enjoy and can be used throughout the classroom. A bulletin board can be set up with a baseball diamond, with each student having his or her own player who can move through the bases. Not only can students keep track of their own RBIs, but they can have a visual reminder of what they have completed as well.

Limitations

One Topic. This menu is best used for one topic with many objectives for in-depth study.

Preparation. With so many choices available to students, teachers should have all materials ready at the beginning of the unit for students to be able to choose any of the activities on the list. This sometimes is a consideration for space in the classroom.

One Free Choice. This menu also only has one opportunity for free choice for students, in the home run section.

Time Considerations

These menus usually are intended for a longer amount of completion time, depending on the number of runs required for a 100%. At most, these are intended for 4 or 5 weeks.

Game Show Menu

"This menu really challenged my students. If one of my students saw another student choosing a more difficult option, they wanted to choose one, too. I had very few students choose to the basic options on this menu. It was wonderful!"

—Sixth-grade science teacher

Description

The Game Show Menu (see Figure 1.5) is the most complex menu. It covers multiple topics or objectives with at least three predetermined choices and a free student choice for each objective. Choices are assigned points based on the levels of Bloom's Revised taxonomy. All choices carry different weights and have different expectations for completion time and effort. A point criterion is set forth that equals 100%. Students must complete at least one activity from each objective in order to reach their goal.

Benefits

Free Choices. This menu allows many choices for students, but if they do not want to complete the offered activities, they can propose their own activity for each objective.

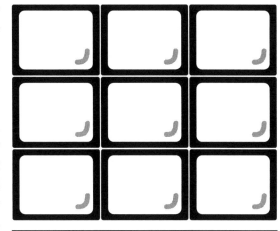

Figure 1.5. Game show menu.

Responsibility. This menu allows students to guarantee their own grades.

Different Learning Levels. It has the flexibility to allow for individualized contracts for different learning levels within the classroom. Each student can create a contract for a certain number of points for his or her 100%.

Objectives Guaranteed. The teacher is guaranteed that the students complete an activity from each objective covered, even if it is at a lower level.

Limitations

Confirm Expectations. The only real limitation here is that students (and parents) must understand the guidelines for completing the menu.

Time Considerations

These menus usually are intended for a longer amount of completion time. Although they can be used as a yearlong menu (each column could be a grading period), they usually are intended for 4–6 weeks.

Free Choice

> "I don't know if I really liked it at first. It's a lot easier to just do the basic stuff and get it over with but when Mrs. [teacher] told us she wanted us to submit at least one free choice, I really got into it! I mean, I could do something I wanted to do? How often do you get to do THAT in school?"
>
> —*Eighth-grade GT student*

With most of the menus, the students are allowed to submit a free choice for their teacher's consideration. Figure 1.6 shows two sample proposal forms that have been used successfully in my classroom. With middle school students, this cuts down greatly on the whining that often accompanies any task given to students. A copy of these forms should be given to each student when the menu is first introduced. The form used is based on the type of menu being presented. For example, if you are using the Tic-Tac-Toe Menu, there is no need to submit a point proposal. A discussion should be held with the students so they understand the expectations of a free choice. I always have a few students who do not want to complete a task on the menu; they are welcome to create their own free choice and submit it for approval. The biggest complainers will not always go to the trouble to complete the form and have it approved, but it is their choice not to do so. The more free choice is used and encouraged, the more students will begin to request it. How the students show their knowledge will begin to shift from teacher-focused to student-designed activities. If students do not want to make a proposal using the proposal form after the teacher has discussed the entire menu and its activities, they can place the unused form in a designated place in the classroom. Others may want to use their form, and it often is surprising who wants to submit a proposal form after hearing about the opportunity!

Proposal forms must be submitted before students begin working on their free-choice products. The teacher then knows what the students are working on and the students know the expectations the teacher has for that product. Once approved, the forms easily can be stapled to the students' menu sheets. The students can refer to it as they develop their free-choice product, and when the grading takes place, the teacher can refer to the agreement for the graded features of the product.

Name: _____   Teacher's Approval: _____

Free-Choice Proposal Form for Point-Based Menu

Points Requested: _____   Points Approved: _____

Proposal Outline

1. What specific topic or idea will you learn about?

2. What criteria should be used to grade it? (Neatness, content, creativity, artistic value, etc.)

3. What will your product look like?

4. What materials will you need from the teacher to create this product?

Name: _____   Teacher's Approval: _____

Free-Choice Proposal Form

Proposal Outline

1. What specific topic or idea will you learn about?

2. What criteria should be used to grade it? (Neatness, content, creativity, artistic value, etc.)

3. What will your product look like?

4. What materials will you need from the teacher to create this product?

Figure 1.6. Sample proposal forms for free choice.

Each part of the proposal form is important and needs to be discussed with students.

- *Name/Teacher's Approval.* The student must submit this form to the teacher for approval. The teacher will carefully review all of the information, send it back to the student for correction, if needed, and then sign the top.

- *Points Requested.* Found only on the point-based menu Free-choice proposal form, this usually is where negotiation needs to take place. Students usually will submit their first request for a very high number (even the 100% goal.) They equate the amount of time something will take with the amount of points it should earn. But, please note, the points are *always* based on the levels of Bloom's Revised taxonomy. For example, a PowerPoint presentation with a vocabulary word quiz would get minimal points, although it may have taken a long time to create. If the students have not been exposed to the levels of Bloom's Revised taxonomy, this can be difficult to explain. You always can refer to the popular "Bloom's Verbs" to help explain the difference between time requirements and higher level activities.

- *Points Approved.* Found only on the point-based menu Free-choice proposal form, this is the final decision recorded by the teacher once the point haggling is finished.

- *Proposal Outline.* This is where the student will tell you everything about the product he or she intends to complete. These questions should be completed in such a way that you can really picture what the student is planning on completing. This also shows you that the student knows what he or she is planning on completing.

  - *What specific topic or idea will you learn about?* Students need to be specific here. It is not acceptable to write *science* or *reading*. This is where they look at the objectives of the product and choose which objective their product demonstrates.

  - *What criteria should be used to grade it?* Although there are rubrics for all of the products that the students might create, it is important for the students to explain what criteria are most important to evaluate the product. The student may indicate that the rubric being used for all of the predetermined products is fine; however, he or she also may want to add other criteria here.

  - *What will your product look like?* It is important for this to be as detailed as possible. If a student cannot express what it will "look like," he or she has probably not given the free-choice plan enough thought.

- *What materials will you need from the teacher to create this product?* This is an important consideration. Sometimes students do not have the means to purchase items for their product. This can be negotiated as well, but if you ask what students may need, they often will develop even grander ideas for their free choice.

CHAPTER 2

How to Use Menus in the Classroom

There are different ways to use instructional menus in the classroom. In order to decide how to implement each menu, the following should be considered: How much prior knowledge of the topic being taught do the students have before the unit or lesson begins, and how much information is readily available for students to obtain on their own? After considering these two questions, there are three customary ways to use menus in the classroom.

Enrichment and Supplemental Activities

Using the menus for enrichment and supplementary activities is the most common way to implement this tool. Usually, the teacher will introduce the menu and the activities at the beginning of the unit. In this case, the students usually do not have a lot of background knowledge and the information about the topic may not be readily available to all students. The teacher then will progress through the content at the normal rate using his or her curricular materials, periodically allowing class and homework time throughout the unit for students to work on their menu choices to supplement a deeper understanding of the lessons being taught. This method is very effective, as it builds in an immediate use for the content the teacher is covering. For example, at the beginning of a unit on mixtures, the teacher many introduce the menu with the explanation that students may not have all of the knowledge to complete all of their choices yet. During the unit, however, more content will be provided and the students will be prepared to work on new choices. If students want to work ahead, they certainly can find the information on their own, but that is not required. Gifted students often see this as a challenge and will begin to investigate concepts mentioned in the menu before the teacher introduces them. This helps build an immense pool of background knowledge before the topic is even discussed in the classroom. As teachers, we fight the battle of having students read ahead or "come to class prepared to discuss." By introducing a menu at the beginning of a unit and allowing students to complete products as instruction progresses, the students naturally investigate the information and come to class prepared without it being a completely separate requirement.

Standard Activities

Another option for using menus in the classroom is to replace certain curricular activities the teacher uses to teach the specified content. In this case, the students may have some limited background knowledge about the content, and information is readily available for them in their classroom resources. The teacher would pick and choose which aspects of the content must be directly taught to the students and which could be appropriately learned and reinforced through product menus. The unit then is designed using both formal instructional lessons and specific menu days where the students will use the menu to reinforce the prior knowledge they already have learned. In order for this option to be effective, the teacher must feel very comfortable with the students' prior knowledge level. Another variation on this method is using the menus to drive center or station activities. Centers have many different functions in the classroom—most importantly reinforcing the instruction that has taken place. Rather than having a set rotation for centers, the teacher could use the menu activities as enrichment or supplementary activities during center time for those students who need more than just reinforcement; centers could be set up with the materials students would need to complete various products.

Mini-Lessons

The third option for menu use is the use of mini-lessons, with the menus driving the accompanying classroom activities. This method is best used when the majority of the students have a lot of prior knowledge about the topic. The teacher would design short 10–15-minute mini-lessons, where students would quickly review or introduce basic concepts that already are familiar to them. The students then are turned loose to choose an activity on the menu to show they understand the concept. The Game Show Menu usually works very well with this method of instruction, as the topics across the top usually lend themselves very well to the mini-lessons. It is important that the students have prior knowledge on the content because the lesson cycle is cut very short in this use of menus. Using menus in this way does not allow the guided practice step of the lesson, as it is assumed the students already understand the information. The teacher simply is reviewing the information and then moving right to the higher levels of Bloom's Revised taxonomy by asking students to create a product. By using the menus in this way, the teacher avoids the "I already know this" glossy looks from his or her students. Another important consideration is the independence level of the students. In order for this use of menus to be effective, students will need to be able to work independently for up to 30 minutes after the mini-lesson. Usually because interest is high in the product they have chosen, this is not a critical issue, but still one worth mentioning as teachers consider how they would like to use various menus in their classroom. Menus can be used in many different ways; all are based on the knowledge and capabilities of the students working on them!

CHAPTER 3

Guidelines for Products

> "... I got to do a play! In math!!"
>
> —*Seventh-grade student*

This chapter outlines the different types of products included in the featured menus, as well as the guidelines and expectations for each. It is very important that students know the expectations of a completed product when they choose to work on it. By discussing these expectations *before* students begin and having the information readily available for students, you will limit frustration on everyone's part.

$1 Contract

Consideration should be given to the cost of creating the products in any menu. The resources available to students vary within a classroom, and students should not be graded on the amount of materials they can purchase to make a product look better. These menus are designed to equalize the resources students have available. The materials for most products are available for less than a dollar and often can be found in a teacher's classroom as part of the classroom supplies. If a product requires

---

$1 Contract

I did not spend more than $1.00 on my _____ .

_____   _____
Student Signature   Date

My child, _____, did not spend more than $1.00 on the product
he or she created.

_____   _____
Parent Signature   Date

Figure 3.1. $1 contract.

materials from the student, there is a $1 contract as part of the product criteria. This is a very important piece in the explanation of the product. First of all, by limiting the amount of money a child can spend, it creates an equal amount of resources for all students. Second, it actually encourages a more creative product. When students are limited by the amount of materials they can readily purchase, they often have to use materials from home in new and unique ways. Figure 3.1 is a sample $1 contract that has been used many times in my classroom with various products.

The Products

Table 3.1 contains a list of the products used in this book. These products were chosen for their flexibility in meeting learning styles, as well as for being products many teachers already encourage in their classroom. They have been arranged by learning style—visual, kinesthetic, or auditory—and each menu has been designed to include products from all of the learning styles. Of course, some of the products may be listed in more than one area depending on how they are presented or implemented. The specific expectations for all of the products are presented in an easy-to-read card format that can be reproduced for students (see Figure 3.2).

The format is convenient for students to have in front of them when they work on their products. These cards also can be laminated and posted

Table 3.1
Products

Visual	Kinesthetic	Auditory
Acrostic	Board Game	Children's Book
Advertisement	Bulletin Board Display	Commercial
Book Cover	Class Game	Game Show
Brochure/Pamphlet	Commercial	Interview
Bulletin Board Display	Concentration Cards	News Report
Cartoon/Comic Strip	Cross-Cut Model	Play/Skit
Children's Book	Diorama	PowerPoint—Speaker
Collage	Drawing	Presentation of Created Product
Cross-Cut Diagram	Flipbook	Puppet
Crossword Puzzle	Folded Quiz Book	Song/Rap
Drawing	Game Show	Speech
Folded Quiz Book	Mobile	Student-Taught Lesson
Greeting Card	Model	Video
Instruction Card	Mural	You Be the Person Presentation
Letter	Play/Skit	
Map	Puppet	
Mind Map	Product Cube	
Newspaper Article	Quiz Board	
Pie Graph	Science Experiment	
Poster	Student-Taught Lesson	
PowerPoint—Stand Alone	Survey	
Questionnaire	Three-Dimensional Timeline	
Quiz Board	Video	
Recipe/Recipe Card		
Scrapbook		
Story		
Survey		
Three Facts and a Fib		
Trading Cards		
Venn Diagram		
WebQuest		
Windowpane		
Worksheet		

on a bulletin board for easy access during classroom work. Some teachers prefer to only give a few product guidelines at a time, while others will provide all of the pages so students feel comfortable venturing out in their free choices. Students enjoy looking at all of the different products and it can stimulate ideas as they peruse the guidelines.

Acrostic	Advertisement	Board Game
• At least 8.5" by 11" • Neatly written or typed • Target word will be written down the left side of the paper • Each descriptive phrase chosen must begin with one of the letters from the target word • Each descriptive phrase chosen must be related to the target word	• At least 8.5" by 11" • A slogan should be included • Color picture of item or service • Include price, if appropriate • Can be developed on the computer	• At least 4 thematic game pieces • At least 25 colored/thematic squares • At least 20 question/activity cards • Include a thematic title on the board • Include a complete set of rules for playing the game • At least the size of an open file folder
Book Cover	**Brochure/Pamphlet**	**Bulletin Board Display**
• Front cover—title, author, image • Cover inside flap—paragraph summary of the book • Back inside flap—brief biography of author with at least five details • Back cover—editorial comments about the book • Spine—title and author	• At least 8.5" by 11" • Must be in three-fold format; front fold has the title and picture • Must have both pictures and written text • Information should be in paragraph form with at least five facts included • Bibliography should be provided as needed • Can be created on computer • Any pictures from Internet must have proper credit	• Must fit within assigned space on bulletin board or wall • Must include at least 10 details • Must have a title • Must have at least five different elements (posters, papers, questions, etc.) • Must have at least one interactive element that engages the reader • $1 contract signed
Cartoon/Comic Strip	**Children's Book**	**Class Game**
• At least 8.5" by 11" • At least six cells • Must have meaningful dialogue • Must include color	• Must have a cover with book's title and student's name as author • Must have at least 10 pages • Each page should have an illustration to accompany the story • Should be neatly written or typed • Can be developed on the computer	• Game will allow everyone in the classroom to participate • Must have only a few, easy-to-understand rules • Should be inventive or a new variation on a current game • Must have multiple question opportunities • Must provide answer key before the game is played • The game must be approved by the teacher before being scheduled for play
Collage	**Commercial**	**Concentration Cards**
• At least 8.5" by 11" • Pictures must be cut neatly from magazines or newspapers (no clip art) • Label items as required in task	• Must be 2–4 minutes in length • Script must be turned in before commercial is presented • Can be presented live to an audience or recorded on a VHS tape or DVD • Should have props or some form of costume(s) • Can include more than one person	• At least 20 index cards (10 matching sets) must be made • Both pictures and words can be used • Information should be placed on just one side of each card • Include an answer key which shows the matches • All cards must be submitted in a carrying bag

Figure 3.2. Product guidelines.

Cross-Cut Model/Diagram	Crossword Puzzle	Diorama
• Must include a scale to show the relationship between the product and the actual item • Must include details about each layer • If creating a model, also must meet the criteria of a model • If creating a diagram, also must meet the criteria of a poster	• At least 20 significant words or phrases should be included • Develop appropriate clues • Include puzzle and answer key • Can be created on the computer	• At least 4" by 5" by 8" • Must be self-standing • All interior space must be covered with relevant pictures and information • Name written on the back in permanent ink • Informational/title card attached to diorama • $1 contract signed
Drawing	**Flipbook**	**Folded Quiz Book**
• Must be at least 8.5" by 11" • Must show what is requested in the task statement • Must include color • Must be neatly drawn by hand • Must have title • Name should be written on the back	• At least 8.5" by 11" folded in half • All information or opinions are supported by facts • Created with the correct number of flaps cut into the top • Color is optional • Name must be written on the back	• At least 8.5" by 11" folded in half • At least 10 questions • Created with the correct number of flaps cut into the top • Questions written or typed neatly on upper flaps • Answers written or typed neatly inside each flap • Color is optional • Name written on the back
Game Show	**Greeting Card**	**Instruction Card**
• Needs an emcee or host. • Must have at least two contestants • There must be at least one regular round and a bonus round • Questions will be content specific • Props can be used, but are not mandatory	• Front—colored pictures, words optional • Front inside—personal note related to topic • Back inside—greeting or saying; must meet product criteria • Back outside—logo, publisher, and price for card	• No larger than 5" by 8" • Created on heavy paper or card • Neatly written or typed • Uses color drawings • Provides instructions stated in the task
Interview	**Letter**	**Map**
• Must have at least eight questions relevant to the topic being studied • Person chosen for interview must be an "expert" and qualified to provide answers based on product criteria • Questions and answers must be neatly written or typed	• Neatly written or typed • Uses proper letter format • At least three paragraphs in length • Must follow type of letter stated in the menu (e.g., friendly, persuasive, informational)	• At least 8.5" by 11" • Accurate information is included • Includes at least 10 relevant locations • Includes compass rose, legend, scale, and key
Mind Map	**Mobile**	**Model**
• At least 8.5" by 11" • Used unlined paper • Must have one central idea • Follow the "no more than four" rule—no more than four words coming from any one word • Should be neatly written or developed using Inspiration	• At least 10 pieces of related information • Includes color and pictures • At least three layers of hanging information • Hangs in a balanced way	• At least 8" by 8" by 12" • Parts of model must be labeled • Should be in scale when appropriate • Must include a title card • Name should be permanently written on model • $1 contract signed

Figure 3.2. Product guidelines, continued.

Mural	News Report	Newspaper Article
• At least 22" x 54" • Must contain at least five pieces of important information • Must have colored pictures • Words are optional, but a title should be included • Name should be written on the back in a permanent way	• Must address the who, what, where, when, why, and how of the topic. • Script of report turned in with project, or before if performance will be "live" • Must be either performed live or recorded on a VHS tape or DVD	• Must be informational in nature • Must follow standard newspaper format • Must include picture with caption that supports article • At least three paragraphs in length • Neatly written or typed
Pie Graph	**Play/Skit**	**Poster**
• Can be created neatly by hand or using computer software • Must have a title • Must have a label for each area or be color coded with a key • Must include the percentages for each area of the graph • Calculations must provided if needed to create the pie graph	• Must be between 5–10 minutes long • Script must be turned in before play is presented • May be presented to an audience or recorded for future showing • Should have props or some form of costume • Can include more than one person	• Should be the size of a standard poster board • Includes at least five pieces of important information • Must have title • Must contain both words and pictures • Name should be written on the back • Bibliography should be included as needed
Power Point—Stand Alone	**Power Point—Speaker**	**Product Cube**
• At least 10 informational slides and one title slide with student's name • No more than 10 words per page • Slides must have color and no more than one graphic per page • Animation is optional, and must not distract from information being presented	• At least 10 informational slides and one title slide with student's name • No more than two words per page • Slides must have color and no more than one graphic per page • Animations are optional but should not distract from information being presented • Presentation should be timed and flow with the speech being given	• All six sides of the cube must be filled with information • Should be neatly written or typed • Name must be printed neatly on the bottom of one of the sides • Should be submitted flat for grading
Puppet	**Questionnaire**	**Quiz Board**
• Puppet should be handmade and must have a moveable mouth • A list of supplies used to make the puppet will be turned in with the puppet • $1 contract signed • If used in a play, all play criteria must be met as well	• Neatly written or typed • At least 10 questions with possible answers, and at least one answer that requires a written response • Questions must be helpful to gathering information on the topic begin studied • At least 15 people must provide answers to questionnaire	• At least five questions • Must have at least five answers • Should use a system with lights to facilitate self-checking • Should be no larger than a poster board • Holiday lights can be used • $1 contract signed
Recipe/Recipe Card	**Scrapbook**	**Song/Rap**
• Must be written neatly or typed on a piece of paper or an index card • Must have a list of ingredients with measurement for each • Must have numbered steps that explain how to make the recipe	• Cover of scrapbook must have a meaningful title and student's name • Must have at least five themed pages • Each page will have at least one meaningful picture • All photos must have captions	• Words must make sense • Can be presented to an audience or taped • Written words will be turned in before performance or with taped song • Should be at least 2 minutes in length

Figure 3.2. Product guidelines, continued.

Speech	Story	Survey
• Must be at least 2 minutes in length • Should not be read from written paper • Note cards can be used • Written speech must be turned in before speech is presented • Voice must be clear, loud, and easy to understand	• Must have all of the elements of a well-written story (setting, characters, conflict, rising action, and resolution) • Must be appropriate length to allow for story elements • Should be neatly written or typed	• Must have at least 5 questions related to the topic • Must include at least one adult that is not your teacher • Although the survey writer may fill in the survey form by asking the questions and writing the exact words given by the respondent, the respondent must sign the survey • Information gathered and conclusions drawn from the survey should be written or presented graphically
Three-Dimensional Timeline	**Three Facts and a Fib**	**Trading Cards**
• Must be no bigger than standard-size poster board • Must be divided into equal time units • Must contain at least 10 important dates and have at least 2 sentences explaining why each date is important • Must have an meaningful, creative object securely attached beside each date to represent that date • Must be able to explain how each object represents each date	• Can be written, typed, or created using Microsoft PowerPoint • Must include exactly four statements: three true statements and one false statement • False statement should not obvious • Brief paragraph should be included that explains why the fib is false	• Include at least 10 cards • Each card should be at least 3" by 5" • Each should have a colored picture • Includes at least three facts on the subject of the card • Cards must have information on both sides • All cards must be submitted in a carrying bag
Venn Diagram	**Video**	**WebQuest**
• At least 8.5" by 11" • Shapes should be thematic and neatly drawn • Must have a title for entire diagram and a title for each section • Must have at least six items in each section of the diagram • Name must be written neatly on the back of the paper	• Use VHS, DVD, or Flash format • Turn in a written plan or story board with project • Students will need to arrange their own video recorder or allow teacher at least 3 days notice for use of video recorder • Covers pertinent information about the project • Name must be written on video label	• Must quest through at least five high-quality Web sites • Web sites should be linked in the document • Can be submitted in a Word or PowerPoint document • At least three questions for each Web site • Must address the topic
Windowpane	**Worksheet**	**You Be the Person Presentation**
• At least 8.5" by 11" unlined paper • At least six squares • Each square must include both a picture and words that should be neatly written or typed • All pictures should be both creative and meaningful • Name should be recorded on the bottom righthand corner of the front of the windowpane	• Must be 8.5" by 11" • Neatly written or typed • Must cover the specific topic or question in detail • Must be creative in design • Must have at least one graphic • An answer key will be turned in with the worksheet	• Take on the role of the person • Cover at least five important facts about the life of the person • Should be between 3 and 5 minutes in length • Script must be turned in before information is presented • Should be presented to an audience with the ability to answer questions while in character • Must have props or some form of costume

Figure 3.2. Product guidelines, continued.

CHAPTER 4

Rubrics

"I frequently end up with more papers and products to grade than with a unit taught in the traditional way. Luckily, the rubric speeds up the process."

—Eighth-grade teacher

The most common reason teachers feel uncomfortable with menus is the need for equal grading. Teachers often feel it is easier to grade the same type of product made by all of the students, rather than grading a large number of different products, none of which looks like any other. The great equalizer for hundreds of different products is a generic rubric that can cover all of the important qualities of an excellent product.

All-Purpose Rubric

Figure 4.1 is an example of a rubric that has been classroom tested with various menus. This rubric can be used with any point value activity presented in a menu. When a menu is presented to students, this rubric can be reproduced on the back of the menu with its guidelines. It also can be given to students to keep in their folder with their product cards so they always know the expectations as they complete products throughout the school year. The first time students see this rubric, it should be explained in detail, especially the last column, Self. It is very important that students self-evaluate their products. This column can provide a unique perspective of the product as it is being graded. *Note*: This rubric was designed to be specific enough that students will know the criteria the teacher is seeking, but general enough that they can still be as creative as they like in the creation of their product. Because all of the point-based menus depend on points that are multiples of 5, the rubric itself has been divided into five areas to make it easier to be more objective with grading.

Student-Taught Lesson Rubric

Although the generic rubric can be used for all activities, there is a special occasion that seems to warrant a special rubric: student-taught lessons. This is a unique situation, with many fine details that must be considered separately.

Student-taught lessons can cause stress for both students and teachers. Teachers often would like to allow students to teach their fellow classmates, but are not comfortable with the grading aspect of the assignment. Rarely do students understand all of the components that go into designing an effective lesson. This student-taught lesson rubric (see Figure 4.2) helps focus the student on the important aspects of a well-designed lesson and allows teachers to make the evaluation a little more subjective.

All-Purpose Product Rubric

Name: _____

Criteria	Excellent (Full Credit)	Good (Half Credit)	Poor (No Credit)	Self
Content: Is the content of the product well chosen?	Content chosen represents the best choice for the product. Graphics are well chosen and related to content.	Information or graphics are related to content, but are not the best choice for the product.	Information or graphics presented do not appear to be related to topic or task.	
Completeness: Is everything included in the product?	All information needed is included. Product meets the product criteria and the criteria of the task as stated.	Some important information is missing. Product meets the product criteria and the criteria of the task as stated.	Most important information is missing. The product does not meet the task or does not meet the product criteria.	
Creativity: Is the product original?	Presentation of information is from a new perspective. Graphics are original. Product includes an element of fun and interest.	Presentation of information is from a new perspective. Graphics are not original. Product has elements of fun and interest.	There is no evidence of new thoughts or perspectives in the product.	
Correctness: Is all of the information included correct?	All information presented in the product is correct and accurate.	N/A	Any portion of the information presented in the product is incorrect.	
Communication: Is the information in the product well communicated?	All information is neat and easy to read. Product is in appropriate format and shows significant effort. Oral presentations are easy to understand and presented with fluency.	Most of the product is neat and easy to read. Product is in appropriate format and shows significant effort. Oral presentations are easy to understand, with some fluency.	The product is not neat and easy to read or the product is not in the appropriate format. It does not show significant effort. Oral presentation was not fluent or easy to understand.	
			Total Grade:	

Figure 4.1. All-purpose product rubric.

Student-Taught Lesson Grading Rubric   Name: _____

Parts of Lesson	Excellent	Good	Fair	Poor	Self
Prepared and Ready: All materials and lesson ready at start of class period, from warm-up to conclusion of lesson.	10 Everything is ready to present.	6 Lesson is present, but small amount of scrambling.	3 Lesson is present, but major scrambling.	0 No lesson ready or missing major components.	
Understanding: Presenters understand the material well. Students understand information presented.	20 All information is correct and in correct format.	12 Presenter understands; 25% of students do not.	4 Presenter understands; 50% of students do not.	0 Presenter is confused.	
Complete: Includes all significant information from section or topic.	15 Includes all important information.	10 Includes most important information.	2 Includes less than 50% of the important information.	0 Information is not related.	
Practice: Includes some way for students to practice or access the information.	20 Practice present; well chosen.	10 Practice present; can be applied effectively.	5 Practice present; not related or best choice.	0 No practice or students are confused.	
Interest/Fun: Most of the class was involved, interested, and participating.	15 Everyone interested and participating.	10 75% actively participating.	5 Less than 50% actively participating.	0 Everyone off task.	
Creativity: Information presented in an imaginative way.	20 Wow, creative! I never would have thought of that!	12 Good ideas!	5 Some good pieces but general instruction.	0 No creativity; all lecture, notes, or worksheet.	
				Total Grade:	

Your Topic/Objective:

Comments:

Don't Forget:
All copy requests and material requests must be made at least 24 hours in advance.

Figure 4.2. Student-taught lesson grading rubric.

Part 2
The Menus

How to Use the Menu Pages

Each menu in this section has:
- an introduction page for the teacher,
- the content menu,
- any specific guidelines, and
- specific activities mentioned in the menu.

Introduction Pages

The introduction pages are meant to provide an overview of each menu. They are divided into five areas.

1. *Objectives Covered Through the Menu and Activities.* This area will list all of the objectives that the menu can address. Menus are arranged in such a way that if students complete the guidelines set forth in the instructions for the menu, all of these objectives will be covered.

2. *Materials Needed by Students for Completion.* For each menu, it is expected that the teacher will provide or students will have access to the following materials: lined paper; glue; crayons, colored pencils, or markers; and blank 8 ½" by 11" white paper. The introduction page also includes a list of additional materials that may be needed by students. Students do have the choice about the menu items they would like to complete, so it is possible that the teacher will not need all of these materials for every student.

3. *Special Notes.* Some menus have special management issues that need to be taken into consideration. This section will share any tips to consider for a specific activity or product.

4. *Time Frame.* Each menu has its own ideal time frame based on its structure, but all work best with at least a one-week time frame. Menus that assess more objectives are better suited to more than 2 weeks. This section will give you an overview about the best time frame for completing the entire menu, as well as options for shorter time periods. If teachers do not have time to devote to an entire menu, they certainly can choose the 1–2-day option for any menu topic students are currently studying.

5. *Suggested Forms.* This is a list of the rubrics that should be available for students as the menus are introduced. If a menu has a free-choice option, the appropriate proposal form also will be listed here.

CHAPTER 5

Numbers and Operations

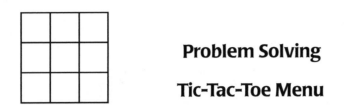

Problem Solving

Tic-Tac-Toe Menu

Objectives Covered Through This Menu and These Activities

- Students will identify different ways to solve problems.
- Students will evaluate different problem-solving techniques and their effectiveness.
- Students will create a method of remembering problem-solving strategies for the future.
- Students will evaluate the reasonableness of answers.

Materials Needed by Students for Completion

- Poster board or large white paper
- Blank index cards (for trading cards)
- Materials for bulletin board display
- DVD or VHS recorder (for commercial)
- Materials for a class game

Special Notes on the Use of This Menu

This menu allows students to create a bulletin board display. Some classrooms may only have one bulletin board, so the teacher can divide the board into sections, or additional classroom wall or hall space can be sectioned off for the creation of these displays. Students can plan their display based on the amount of space they are assigned.

This menu gives students the opportunity to create a commercial. Although students enjoy producing their own videos, there often are difficulties obtaining the equipment and scheduling the use of the video recorder. This can be modified by allowing students to act out the commercial (like a play) or, if students have the technology, they may wish to produce a Webcam or Flash version of their commercial.

Students also are given the opportunity to create a game for the class. The length of the game is not stated in the product guidelines, so the teacher can determine what works best. It may be good to have students start with shorter games and work up to longer games with a review focus.

Time Frame

- 2–3 weeks—Students are given the menu as the unit is started. As the teacher presents lessons throughout the week, he or she should refer back to the menu options associated with that content. The teacher will go over all of the options for that content and have students place checkmarks in the boxes that represent the activities they are most interested in completing. As teaching continues over the next 2–3 weeks, activities chosen and completed should make a column or row. When students complete this pattern, they have completed one activity from each content area, learning style, or level of Bloom's, depending on the design of the menu.

- 1 week—At the start of the unit, the teacher chooses the three activities he or she feels are most valuable for the students. Stations can be set up in the classroom. These three activities are available for student choice throughout the week as regular instruction takes place.
- 1–2 days—The teacher chooses an activity from the menu to use with the entire class.

Suggested Forms

- All-purpose rubric
- Free-choice proposal form

Name:_____ Date:_____

Problem Solving

☐ *Evaluating Problem-Solving Strategies* Develop a brochure that explains the different problem-solving strategies and how a student could decide which strategy is best for him or her.	☐ *Evaluating Reasonableness* Students usually solve a word problem and write down the answer without considering if the answer is reasonable or possible. Create a class lesson to help your classmates become more proficient at evaluating their answers.	☐ *Using Problem Solving in the Future* Create a set of trading cards for the various problem-solving strategies. Include a real-world example on each card.
☐ *Using Problem Solving in the Future* Create a song or rap that teaches the different problem-solving strategies. Teach it to your classmates!	☐ **Free Choice: Evaluating Problem-Solving Strategies** (Fill out your proposal form before beginning the free choice!)	☐ *Evaluating Reasonableness* Create a folded quiz book with at least eight different word problems, each with one reasonable answer and one that is not a reasonable answer. The purpose of your quiz is not to calculate the correct answer, but to determine which answer is the most reasonable.
☐ *Evaluating Reasonableness* Create a class game that focuses not on the correct answer to word problems, but rather whether an answer is reasonable.	☐ *Using Problem Solving in the Future* Create a bulletin board display for each of the different problem-solving strategies you have used in the past. Include examples of each in your display.	☐ *Evaluating Problem-Solving Strategies* Although there are many problem-solving techniques, everyone has a preference. Which technique do you find the most helpful? Create a commercial for this technique and include specific reasons why you feel that strategy is the best.

Check the boxes you plan to complete. They should form a tic-tac-toe across or down.

All products are due by: _____.

Fractions and Decimals

List Menu

Objectives Covered Through This Menu and These Activities
- Students will convert between fractions and decimals.
- Students will add, subtract, multiply, and divide fractions and decimals.

Materials Needed by Students for Completion
- Poster board or large white paper
- Socks (for puppets)
- Paper bags (for puppets)
- Graph paper or Internet access (for crossword puzzle)
- Blank index cards (for trading cards and concentration cards)
- Materials for board games (e.g., folders, colored cards)
- Materials for class game
- Microsoft PowerPoint or other slideshow software

Special Notes on the Use of This Menu
Students also are given the opportunity to create a game for the class. The length of the game is not stated in the product guidelines, so the teacher can determine what works best. It may be good to have students start with shorter games and work up to longer games with a review focus.

Time Frame
- 1–2 weeks—Students are given the menu as the unit is started and the guidelines and point expectations are discussed. Students usually will need to earn 100 points for 100%, although there is an opportunity for extra credit if the teacher would like to use another target number. Because this menu covers one topic in depth, the teacher will go over all of the options on the menu and have students place checkmarks in the boxes next to the activities they are most interested in completing. Teachers will need to set aside a few moments to sign the agreement at the bottom of the page with each student. As instruction continues, activities are completed by students and submitted for grading.
- 1–2 days—The teacher chooses an activity or product from an objective to use with the entire class during that lesson time.

Suggested Forms
- All-purpose rubric
- Free-choice proposal form for point-based products

Name:_____ Date:_____

Fractions and Decimals

Guidelines:
1. You may complete as many of the activities listed within the time period.
2. You may choose any combination of activities.
3. Your goal is 100 points. You may earn up to _____ points extra credit.
4. You may be as creative as you like within the guidelines listed below.
5. You must show your plan to your teacher by _____.
6. Activities may be turned in at any time during the working time period. They will be graded and recorded on this sheet as you continue to work, so keep it safe!

Plan to Do	Activity to Complete	Point Value	Date Completed	Points Earned
	Write and perform a play about a fraction family that has decided to convert to decimals, hoping the children in their neighborhood will like them better in their new form.	30		
	Create a fraction puppet and use it to explain how to convert fractions to decimals.	30		
	Create a number crossword puzzle for different fraction and decimal problems.	20		
	Create a poster with the decimal equivalents of the most common fractions. Include a drawing of the decimals and fractions to support your equivalents.	15		
	Create a set of concentration cards for fractions and their corresponding decimal equivalents.	15		
	Create a 10-flap flipbook with decimals on the top flaps. Place a least 3 or 4 equivalent fractions for each decimal inside each flap.	20		
	Make a *Fractions Are Fun and Decimals Are Delicious!* children's book that shows how to complete word problems using fractions and decimals, as well as how to convert between the two. Include examples that would interest your young readers.	30		
	Create a Venn diagram that compares and contrasts decimals and fractions.	20		
	Create a set of trading cards for all of the decimals in the eighths family. Include their equivalent fractions, facts about them, and at least one drawing.	25		
	Design a class game that allows your classmates to practice their decimal and fraction skills.	30		
	Create a PowerPoint presentation that shows how to add, subtract, multiply, and divide fractions and decimals.	25		
	Submit your free-choice proposal form for a product of your choice.	15–30		
	Total number of points you are planning to earn.	**Total points earned:**		

I am planning to complete _____ activities that could earn up to a total of _____ points.

Teacher's initials _____ Student's signature _____

Adding and Subtracting Fractions

20-50-80 Menu

Objectives Covered Through This Menu and These Activities

- Students will complete word problems that require addition and subtraction of fractions, including mixed numbers and improper fractions.
- Students will recognize real-world applications of the addition and subtraction of fractions.

Materials Needed by Students for Completion

- Poster board or large white paper
- Materials for board games (e.g., folders, colored cards)
- Materials for manipulatives and model of subtraction of fractions
- Materials for a student-designed cooking show
- DVD or VHS recorder (for cooking show)

Special Notes on the Use of This Menu

This menu gives students the opportunity to create a cooking show. Some students may want to perform their show live while others may want to record their performance instead. The teacher can give students both options and allow them to choose what works best.

Time Frame

- 1–2 weeks—Students are given the menu as the unit is started, and the teacher discusses all of the product options on the menu. As the different options are discussed, students will choose products that add to a total of 100 points. As the lessons progress through the week(s), the teacher and students refer back to the menu options associated with the content being taught.
- 1–2 days—The teacher chooses an activity or product from the menu to use with the entire class.

Suggested Forms

- All-purpose rubric
- Student-taught lesson rubric (can be used for the cooking show)
- Free-choice proposal form for point based projects

Adding and Subtracting Fractions

Directions: Choose two activities from the menu below. The activities must total 100 points. Place a checkmark next to each box to show which activities you will complete. All activities must be completed by _____.

20 Points

❏ Design a worksheet that shows how to add and subtract fractions. Include mixed numbers and improper fractions, as well as multiple practice problems for your classmates.

❏ Create a brochure that provides instructions for adding and subtracting improper fractions and mixed numbers.

50 Points

❏ Make a fraction board game that tests your classmates' knowledge of adding and subtracting fractions using real-world word problems.

❏ Students often have trouble when completing a fraction subtraction problem that requires borrowing. Create a model that uses manipulatives to help these students better understand the process of borrowing.

❏ Write a children's book about the number 24 and its job as a popular and busy common denominator used by many mixed and improper fractions.

❏ Free choice—prepare a proposal form and submit your idea for approval.

80 Points

❏ Create your own cooking show (or play) in which you prepare a food for the audience. Your assistants did not bring enough materials and have only provided you with a ¼-cup measuring cup and ½ teaspoon in order to make your recipe. Have fun preparing your dish for your audience; be sure and explain how you can make your measurements using these smaller measuring tools.

❏ Obtain a map or floor plan for your school. Using measurements and scale, create a model of your school building. Include your measurements and conversions with your model.

Integers

20-50-80 Menu

Objectives Covered Through This Menu and These Activities

- Students will identify real-world examples of addition, subtraction, multiplication, and division of integers.

Materials Needed by Students for Completion

- Poster board or large white paper
- Scrapbooking materials
- Newspapers
- Magazines (for collage)
- Microsoft PowerPoint or other slideshow software
- Materials for bulletin board display

Special Notes on the Use of This Menu

This menu allows students to create a bulletin board display. Some classrooms may only have one bulletin board, so the teacher can divide the board into sections, or additional classroom wall or hall space can be sectioned off for the creation of these displays. Students can plan their display based on the amount of space they are assigned.

Time Frame

- 1–2 weeks—Students are given the menu as the unit is started, and the teacher discusses all of the product options on the menu. As the different options are discussed, students will choose products that add to a total of 100 points. As the lessons progress through the week(s), the teacher and students refer back to the menu options associated with the content being taught.
- 1–2 days—The teacher chooses an activity or product from the menu to use with the entire class.

Suggested Forms

- All-purpose rubric
- Free-choice proposal form for point-based projects

Integers

Directions: Choose two activities from the menu below. The activities must total 100 points. Place a checkmark next to each box to show which activities you will complete. All activities must be completed by _____.

---

20 Points

❏ Create an integer song or rap that can help students remember how the signs of integers change in different types of problems.

❏ Design a poster that shows pictorial examples of all of the different types of integer problems.

---

50 Points

❏ Create a brochure that shows how to complete calculations with integers. Be sure to include examples of word problems readers might encounter!

❏ Design a bulletin board display that explains how to create quality addition, subtraction, multiplication, and division word problems using integers.

❏ The idea that two negatives do not make a positive is not always true in mathematics. After investigating the interaction of integers, design a PowerPoint presentation to show how they interact differently depending on the type of problem.

❏ Using the newspaper, locate at least three stories that can be used to create four integer word problems. Create a scrapbook to show the stories, word problems, and the solutions. Be sure to include addition, subtraction, multiplication, and division, as well as positive and negative integers.

---

80 Points

❏ Create a collage for the number 36 with at least 25 different integer calculations, including addition, subtraction, multiplication, and division, that have 36 as their answer. Be creative in your integer equations; try not to make them sequential.

❏ Free choice—prepare a proposal form and submit your idea for approval.

Order of Operations

Tic-Tac-Toe Menu

Objectives Covered Through This Menu and These Activities

- Students will explain to others how to use the acronym PEMDAS when solving order of operation problems.
- Students will brainstorm and solve multiple-step problems that require the use of order of operations.

Materials Needed by Students for Completion

- Poster board or large white paper
- Materials for bulletin board display
- Coat hangers (for mobile)
- Index cards (for mobile)
- String (for mobile)

Special Notes on the Use of This Menu

This menu allows students to create a bulletin board display. Some classrooms may only have one bulletin board, so the teacher can divide the board into sections, or additional classroom wall or hall space can be sectioned off for the creation of these displays. Students can plan their display based on the amount of space they are assigned.

Time Frame

- 2–3 weeks—Students are given the menu as the unit is started. As the teacher presents lessons throughout the week, he or she should refer back to the menu options associated with that content. The teacher will go over all of the options for that content and have students place checkmarks in the boxes that represent the activities they are most interested in completing. As teaching continues over the next 2–3 weeks, activities chosen and completed should make a column or row. When students complete this pattern, they have completed one activity from each content area, learning style, or level of Bloom's, depending on the design of the menu.
- 1 week—At the start of the unit, the teacher chooses the three activities he or she feels are most valuable for the students. Stations can be set up in the classroom. These three activities are available for student choice throughout the week as regular instruction takes place.

- 1–2 days—The teacher chooses an activity from the menu to use with the entire class.

Suggested Forms
- All-purpose rubric
- Student-taught lesson rubric
- Free-choice proposal form

Order of Operations

☐ *Please Excuse Who?* Rewrite the "Hokey Pokey" song to teach the order of operations to your classmates. Be ready to get up and have the class dance with you as you complete a problem of your choice!	☐ *It's as Easy as 1, 2, 3!* Create examples of five different order of operation problems students have trouble computing. Create a bulletin board display that shows the problems and strategies for completing them correctly.	☐ *Know Your Goal!* Choose any prime number greater than 11. Create a mobile for your number that includes multiple complex methods of obtaining your target number.
☐ *Know Your Goal!* You have been given the goal number of 7. Brainstorm at least 10 different operation sequences using all of the functions of PEMDAS to achieve your goal number. Use a poster to show the different ways you achieved your goal.	☐ **Free Choice: Teaching PEMDAS** (Fill out your proposal form before beginning the free choice!)	☐ *It's as Easy as 1, 2, 3!* Create a children's book that makes order of operations fun, understandable, and applicable to student's real lives. Include at least two creative problems in your book.
☐ *It's as Easy as 1, 2, 3!* Create an order of operations brochure that explains how to solve complex multiple-step order of operations problems. Include various examples to assist your explanation.	☐ *Know Your Goal!* Your age is your goal number. Create Three Facts and a Fib for your target number using order of operations. The operation statements must include all of the PEMDAS statements and at least eight different calculations.	☐ *Please Excuse Who?* Create a short class lesson that teaches students alternate ways to remember the order of operations. Allow plenty of practice on both simple and complex examples.

Check the boxes you plan to complete. They should form a tic-tac-toe across or down.

All products are due by: _____.

Mean, Median, Mode, and Range

List Menu

Objectives Covered Through This Menu and These Activities

- Students will identify real-world examples of mean, median, mode, and range.
- Students will calculate mean, median, mode, and range for given or obtained sets of data.

Materials Needed by Students for Completion

- Poster board or large white paper
- Newspapers
- Microsoft PowerPoint or other slideshow software
- Internet access (for WebQuest)
- Materials for board games (folders, colored cards, etc.)

Special Notes on the Use of This Menu

This menu allows students to create a WebQuest. There are multiple versions and templates for WebQuests available on the Internet. Teachers may decide whether to specify a certain format or allow students to create one of their own choosing.

Time Frame

- 1–2 weeks—Students are given the menu as the unit is started and the guidelines and point expectations are discussed. Students usually will need to earn 100 points for 100%, although there is an opportunity for extra credit if the teacher would like to use another target number. Because this menu covers one topic in depth, the teacher will go over all of the options on the menu and have students place checkmarks in the boxes next to the activities they are most interested in completing. Teachers will need to set aside a few moments to sign the agreement at the bottom of the page with each student. As instruction continues, activities are completed by students and submitted for grading.
- 1–2 days—The teacher chooses an activity or product from an objective to use with the entire class during that lesson time.

Suggested Forms

- All-purpose rubric
- Free-choice proposal form for point-based products

Name:_____ Date:_____

Mean, Median, Mode, and Range

Guidelines:

1. You may complete as many of the activities listed within the time period.
2. You may choose any combination of activities.
3. Your goal is 100 points. You may earn up to _____ points extra credit.
4. You may be as creative as you like within the guidelines listed below.
5. You must show your plan to your teacher by _____.
6. Activities may be turned in at any time during the working time period. They will be graded and recorded on this sheet as you continue to work, so keep it safe!

Plan to Do	Activity to Complete	Point Value	Date Completed	Points Earned
	Using the sports section of the newspaper, research the statistics of at least 20 players of one sport. After gathering the data, record the mean, median, and mode for the players on either a poster or PowerPoint presentation. Explain what each number means to the sport.	30		
	Consider the career you wish to pursue when you graduate from college. Research the various salaries of this profession based on experience and time in the field. Create a poster that shows your research. After determining the mean, median, mode, and range for the salaries, share which method of calculation you would prefer to determine your starting salary.	25		
	Create a windowpane for the key statistical concepts we are discussing.	15		
	Choose a company and use the Internet to research the mean, median, mode, and range of its stocks of the past 52-week period. The Executive Board of this company has asked for a report on the company's success. Create a PowerPoint presentation that shares the information in the most positive light. Present it to the class.	30		
	Create a flipbook for mean, median, mode, and range. Share an example of each and how to calculate each one.	15		
	Write and perform a song or rap to help your classmates remember the difference between mean, median, and mode.	20		
	Create a questionnaire to gather data about three popular questions, and have at least 10 people complete it. Present the mean, median, and mode of your data.	20		
	Design a WebQuest that visits various sites that contain data. Have your classmates complete the WebQuest and use the data in a meaningful way to calculate means, modes, and ranges.	25		
	Create a board game for mean, median, mode, and range. Focus on real-world applications of each and how to calculate all four.	20		
	Are you the mean, median, or mode in your classroom? Choose one physical aspect of your classmates (e.g., height, diameter of head, length of hands) and, after recording the measurements on a data table, calculate and show the mean, median, and mode of your gathered information.	25		
	Write a worksheet with real-world examples and problems for mean, mode, and range.	15		
	Submit your free-choice proposal form for a product of your choice.			
	Total number of points you are planning to earn.	**Total points earned:**		

I am planning to complete _____ activities that could earn up to a total of _____ points.

Teacher's initials _____ Student's signature _____

Ratios

Tic-Tac-Toe Menu

Objectives Covered Through This Menu and These Activities

- Students will use ratios to describe proportional situations.
- Students will represent ratios with models, fractions, and decimals.
- Students will use ratios to make predictions in proportional situations.

Materials Needed by Students for Completion

- Poster board or large white paper
- Blank index cards (for concentration cards)
- Newspaper and magazines (for collage)
- Materials for bulletin board display
- Microsoft PowerPoint or other slideshow software
- Materials for board games (e.g., folders, colored cards)
- Scrapbooking materials

Special Notes on the Use of this Menu

This menu allows students to create a bulletin board display. Some classrooms may only have one bulletin board, so the teacher can divide the board into sections, or additional classroom wall or hall space can be sectioned off for the creation of these displays. Students can plan their display based on the amount of space they are assigned.

Time Frame

- 2–3 weeks—Students are given the menu as the unit is started. As the teacher presents lessons throughout the week, he or she should refer back to the menu options associated with that content. The teacher will go over all of the options for that content and have students place checkmarks in the boxes that represent the activities they are most interested in completing. As teaching continues over the next 2–3 weeks, activities chosen and completed should make a column or row. When students complete this pattern, they have completed one activity from each content area, learning style, or level of Bloom's, depending on the design of the menu.
- 1 week—At the start of the unit, the teacher chooses the three activities he or she feels are most valuable for the students. Stations can be

set up in the classroom. These three activities are available for student choice throughout the week as regular instruction takes place.

- 1–2 days—The teacher chooses an activity from the menu to use with the entire class.

Suggested Forms

- All-purpose rubric
- Free-choice proposal form

Ratios

☐ Everyday Ratios Your classmates can calculate ratios, but can they predict them accurately? Create a game show that has participants predicting ratios that can be observed every day.	**☐ Can Ratios Predict the Future?** Create a survey to gather information about a recent controversial topic in the news. After surveying 10 people, use this information to predict how a larger sample size might respond. Put your prediction to the test and create a speech to share the results from your prediction.	**☐ Ratios, Fractions, and Decimals, Oh My!** Create a set of concentration cards that asks students to find matching ratios, fractions, and decimals.
☐ Ratios, Fractions, and Decimals, Oh My! Search through newspapers and magazines to find examples of objects that can be expressed as ratios, fractions, or decimals. Create a collage of the different examples. Write three numbers represented by each one: the ratio, fraction, and decimal.	**☐ Free Choice: Everyday Ratios** (Fill out your proposal form before beginning the free choice!)	**☐ Can Ratios Predict the Future?** You have been given the task to figure out the number of living creatures smaller than 1 cm found on the football field. Create a plan, make your measurements, and then determine your final prediction. Share your results through a bulletin board display.
☐ Can Ratios Predict the Future? Choose your favorite professional team (or athlete) and research its statistics. Prepare a poster or PowerPoint presentation about the statistics and their meanings. Include a precise prediction about the team's performance in its next game.	**☐ Ratios, Fractions, and Decimals, Oh My!** Design a board game for practicing the conversions between ratios, fractions, and decimals. Please include an answer key so players can double check their responses.	**☐ Everyday Ratios** Create a scrapbook of ratios that can be found in our daily lives. Be creative in what you choose as examples.

Check the boxes you plan to complete. They should form a tic-tac-toe across or down.

All products are due by: _____.

Scientific Notation

20-50-80 Menu

Objectives Covered Through This Menu and These Activities

- Students will understand the real-world applications of scientific notation.
- Students will write numbers in scientific notation using both positive and negative exponents.

Materials Needed by Students for Completion

- Poster board or large white paper
- Blank index cards (for card game)
- Large lined index cards (for instruction card)
- Magazines (for collage)
- Internet access (for WebQuest)

Special Notes on the Use of This Menu

This menu allows students to create a WebQuest. There are multiple versions and templates for WebQuests available on the Internet. Teachers may decide whether to specify a certain format or allow students to create one of their own choosing.

Time Frame

- 1–2 weeks—Students are given the menu as the unit is started, and the teacher discusses all of the product options on the menu. As the different options are discussed, students will choose products that add to a total of 100 points. As the lessons progress through the week(s), the teacher and students refer back to the menu options associated with the content being taught.
- 1–2 days—The teacher chooses an activity or product from the menu to use with the entire class.

Suggested Forms

- All-purpose rubric
- Free-choice proposal form for point-based projects

Scientific Notation

Directions: Choose two activities from the menu below. The activities must total 100 points. Place a checkmark next to each box to show which activities you will complete. All activities must be completed by _____.

---

20 Points

❏ Create a place value card game that would assist players in writing numbers in scientific notation.

❏ Design an instruction card that details how to write numbers in scientific notation. Include instructions for both positive and negative exponents, as well as examples to support your instructions.

---

50 Points

❏ Create a collage with photos that represent objects that would be measured using scientific notation. Label examples with approximate realistic measurements. Be sure to include examples of both positive and negative exponents.

❏ Create a cross-cut model of an object that needs scientific notation for its scale based on its size. Label the different parts of your model using the notation.

❏ Create Three Facts and a Fib about how scientific notation is used in our daily lives.

❏ Free choice—prepare a proposal form and submit your idea for approval.

---

80 Points

❏ Create a WebQuest that takes participants through the world of scientific notation. It should include sites with examples of objects measured in scientific notation and practice in writing numbers in scientific notation.

❏ Scientific notation can be used for any number, except perhaps numbers 1–9. Writing numbers using this method can make calculations and writing of the number easier. The United States is thinking of requiring all numbers greater than 9 and less than 1 to now be expressed only in scientific notation. Consider this idea and write a newspaper article either in support of or against this new idea. Be sure to discuss both sides of the issue using examples before trying to persuade the reader of your opinion.

Square Roots

20-50-80 Menu

Objectives Covered Through This Menu and These Activities

- Students will estimate and calculate square roots without a calculator.
- Students will communicate practical uses for the square root in our daily lives.

Materials Needed by Students for Completion

- Poster board or large white paper
- Materials to create manipulatives
- Graph paper or Internet access (for crossword puzzle)
- Materials for bulletin board display
- Internet access (for WebQuest)
- Scrapbooking materials

Special Notes on the Use of This Menu

This menu allows students to create a WebQuest. There are multiple versions and templates for WebQuests available on the Internet. Teachers may decide whether to specify a certain format or allow students to create one of their own choosing.

This menu also allows students to create a bulletin board display. Some classrooms may only have one bulletin board, so the teacher can divide the board into sections, or additional classroom wall or hall space can be sectioned off for the creation of these displays. Students can plan their display based on the amount of space they are assigned.

Time Frame

- 1–2 weeks—Students are given the menu as the unit is started, and the teacher discusses all of the product options on the menu. As the different options are discussed, students will choose products that add to a total of 100 points. As the lessons progress through the week(s), the teacher and students refer back to the menu options associated with the content being taught.
- 1–2 days—The teacher chooses an activity or product from the menu to use with the entire class.

Suggested Forms

- All-purpose rubric
- Free-choice proposal form for point-based projects

Square Roots

Directions: Choose two activities from the menu below. The activities must total 100 points. Place a checkmark next to each box to show which activities you will complete. All activities must be completed by _____.

---

20 Points

❏ Create a model or set of manipulatives that can be used to show square roots. Include instructions for using the manipulatives.

❏ Create an instruction card that explains in your own words how to calculate the square root of a number without using a calculator.

---

50 Points

❏ Create a number crossword puzzle (where all of the answers are numbers) for calculating the square root of various numbers rounded to the nearest thousandth.

❏ Write and perform a song or rap about why a student should learn how to calculate square roots.

❏ Design a bulletin board display that shows how to solve square root problems, as well as sample word problems that require this skill to calculate the answer.

❏ Create a WebQuest that takes visitors to at least three different sites where they can try their hand at solving different types of square root problems.

---

80 Points

❏ Being able to calculate the square root of a number is expected in many different types of mathematical situations. Create a scrapbook of situations and sample problems where the calculation of the square root of a number is needed in our daily lives.

❏ Free choice—prepare a proposal form and submit your idea for approval.

CHAPTER 6

Geometry

Angles

20-50-80 Menu

Objectives Covered Through This Menu and These Activities

- Students will use angle measurements to classify angles as acute, obtuse, or right.
- Students will classify angle pairs as complementary or supplementary.

Materials Needed by Students for Completion

- Poster board or large white paper
- Magazines (for collage)
- Blank index cards (for trading cards and mobile)
- Coat hangers (for mobile)
- String (for mobile)
- Microsoft PowerPoint or other slideshow software

Time Frame

- 1–2 weeks—Students are given the menu as the unit is started, and the teacher discusses all of the product options on the menu. As the different options are discussed, students will choose products that add to a total of 100 points. As the lessons progress through the week(s), the teacher and students refer back to the menu options associated with the content being taught.
- 1–2 days—The teacher chooses an activity or product from the menu to use with the entire class.

Suggested Forms

- All-purpose rubric
- Student-taught lesson rubric
- Free-choice proposal form for point-based projects

Angles

Directions: Choose two activities from the menu below. The activities must total 100 points. Place a checkmark next to each box to show which activities you will complete. All activities must be completed by _____.

20 Points

❏ Create a collage of examples of acute, obtuse, and right angles we see around us. Label the different angles in each picture.

❏ Create a set of trading cards for each type of angle, including complementary and supplementary angles. Examples should contain ones you could see on a daily basis.

50 Points

❏ Make a mobile for acute, obtuse, and right angles with photos of at least two examples of each angle that can be observed on a daily basis. Using a protractor to measure the angles to prove its classification, share the measurements as part of your mobile.

❏ Design a how-to PowerPoint presentation that shows how to classify the different types of angles, including complementary and supplementary, using a protractor. Be sure to include how to use a protractor in your presentation.

❏ Create a song or rap about complementary and supplementary angles and how to identify them.

❏ Free choice—prepare a proposal form and submit your idea for approval.

80 Points

❏ A new game show called "It's All About the Angle!" is being produced by a local television station, and they want a local student to create the game. Design your version of this show using classmates as contestants.

❏ Create a lesson that shows students how to use a compass to construct each type of angle, as well as how to create an angle's complement or supplement.

Solid Figures

20-50-80 Menu

Objectives Covered Through This Menu and These Activities

- Students will determine properties of pyramids, cones, prisms, and cylinders.
- Students will identify real-world examples of geometric solids.

Materials Needed by Students for Completion

- Poster board or large white paper
- Blank index cards (for trading cards and mobile)
- Coat hangers (for mobile)
- String (for mobile)
- Boxes for diorama
- Scrapbooking materials
- Internet access (for WebQuest)
- Project cube template

Special Notes on the Use of This Menu

This menu allows students to create a WebQuest. There are multiple versions and templates for WebQuests available on the Internet. Teachers may decide whether to specify a certain format or allow students to create one of their own choosing.

Time Frame

- 1–2 weeks—Students are given the menu as the unit is started, and the teacher discusses all of the product options on the menu. As the different options are discussed, students will choose products that add to a total of 100 points. As the lessons progress through the week(s), the teacher and students refer back to the menu options associated with the content being taught.
- 1–2 days—The teacher chooses an activity or product from the menu to use with the entire class.

Suggested Forms

- All-purpose rubric
- Free-choice proposal form for point-based projects

Solid Figures

Directions: Choose two activities from the menu below. The activities must total 100 points. Place a checkmark next to each box to show which activities you will complete. All activities must be completed by _____.

---

20 Points

❏ Create a set of trading cards for all of the geometric shapes and solids.

❏ After grouping similar geometric solids together, create a mobile for the solids that includes an example of each and its properties.

---

50 Points

❏ Complete a cube with one geometric solid on each side. Give a real-world example of the shape, as well as the properties that define it.

❏ Create a model or diorama of your bedroom using examples from all of the geometric shapes. Create a key that tells the shapes that form each object.

❏ Design a scrapbook with pictures of different geometric solids that can be found in your neighborhood. Be creative in where you look for your shapes, from signs, to art, to architecture.

❏ Free choice—prepare a proposal form and submit your idea for approval.

---

80 Points

❏ Create a sculpture using at least three different-sized pyramids, two cones, three prisms, and one cylinder that you can find at home. After creating your sculpture, write a story that tells about the sculpture and its background.

❏ Design a WebQuest that exposes users to photographs and examples of structures and sculptures created to represent geometric solids. Focus your questions on identifying the solids represented and their properties.

Solid Figures Cube

Complete a cube with one geometric solid on each side. Give a real-world example of the shape, as well as the properties that define it. Use this pattern or create your own cube.

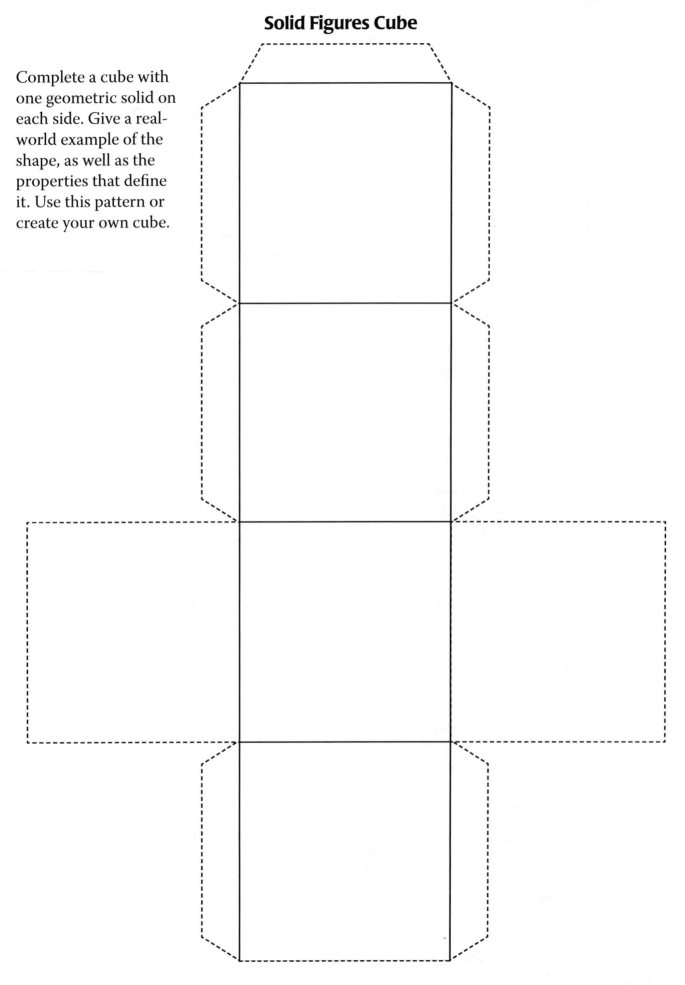

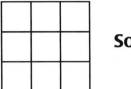

Solids and Spatial Reasoning

Tic-Tac-Toe Menu

Objectives Covered Through This Menu and These Activities

- Students will sketch solids from various views including front, back, top, and sides.
- Students will identify pyramids, cones, prisms, and cylinders and their properties.
- Students will show how space figures are used in architectural design.

Materials Needed by Students for Completion

- Materials for the cross-cut model
- DVD or VHS recorder (for commercial)
- Poster board or large white paper
- Coat hangers (for mobile)
- Index cards (for mobile)
- String (for mobile)
- Microsoft PowerPoint or other slideshow software
- Solid figures for sculpture

Special Notes on the Use of This Menu

This menu gives students the opportunity to create a commercial. Although students enjoy producing their own videos, there often are difficulties obtaining the equipment and scheduling the use of the video recorder. This can be modified by allowing students to act out the commercial (like a play) or, if students have the technology, they may wish to produce a Webcam or Flash version of their commercial.

Time Frame

- 2–3 weeks—Students are given the menu as the unit is started. As the teacher presents lessons throughout the week, he or she should refer back to the menu options associated with that content. The teacher will go over all of the options for that content and have students place checkmarks in the boxes that represent the activities they are most interested in completing. As teaching continues over the next 2–3 weeks, activities chosen and completed should make a column or row. When students complete this pattern, they have completed one activity from each content area, learning style, or level of Bloom's, depending on the design of the menu.

- 1 week—At the start of the unit, the teacher chooses the three activities he or she feels are most valuable for the students. Stations can be set up in the classroom. These three activities are available for student choice throughout the week as regular instruction takes place.
- 1–2 days—The teacher chooses an activity from the menu to use with the entire class.

Suggested Forms

- All-purpose rubric
- Free-choice proposal form

Solids and Spatial Reasoning

☐ *Identifying Solid Figures* Gather at least four different examples of cylinders, pyramids, cones, and prisms (at least 16 examples in total) that can be found in your home. Label each example with the type of figure.	☐ *Solids From Various Views* Create a cross-cut model for each of the different types of solid figures. Include a poster for your figures that also shows all of the exterior views: top, side, front, and back.	☐ *Solid Figures* Architecture often is dependent on geometric figures. Locate a picture of a great castle of your choice and analyze its structure and dependence on space figures. Create a commercial for your own castle-building business that only uses geometric solids in its designs.
☐ *Solid Figures* As an architect, you create whatever the client wants. Your present client has asked for a home designed only from solid figures. Using solid figures, create a model home for your client. Also include a drawing of the front, sides, and back of the house.	**Free Choice: Identifying Solid Figures** (Fill out your proposal form before beginning the free choice!)	☐ *Solids From Various Views* Choose two solid figures and make a poster that shows these figures from the front, top, back, and sides.
☐ *Solids From Various Views* Create a "Mystery Figure" PowerPoint presentation in which you show different views of various solid figures from the top, front, side, or back so the users of the PowerPoint can guess the figure.	☐ *Solid Figures* Create a mobile for the different solid figures. For each, include the name, a written description, a net for each shape, and a small household example.	☐ *Identifying Solid Figures* Gather at least three examples of different-sized cylinders, pyramids, cones, and prisms. Create a sculpture out of all of the objects. Write a paragraph about your sculpture and the different figures found in it.

Check the boxes you plan to complete. They should form a tic-tac-toe across or down.

All products are due by: _____.

Circles

20-50-80 Menu

Objectives Covered Through This Menu and These Activities

- Students will calculate the radius, diameter, and circumference of a circle.
- Students will understand the relationship between the measurements of a radius and circumference.

Materials Needed by Students for Completion

- Magazines (for collage)
- Poster board or large white paper
- Microsoft PowerPoint or other slideshow software
- Internet access (for epicenter triangulation)

Time Frame

- 1–2 weeks—Students are given the menu as the unit is started, and the teacher discusses all of the product options on the menu. As the different options are discussed, students will choose products that add to a total of 100 points. As the lessons progress through the week(s), the teacher and students refer back to the menu options associated with the content being taught.
- 1–2 days—The teacher chooses an activity or product from the menu to use with the entire class.

Suggested Forms

- All-purpose rubric
- Free-choice proposal form for point-based projects

Circles

Directions: Choose two activities from the menu below. The activities must total 100 points. Place a checkmark next to each box to show which activities you will complete. All activities must be completed by

_____.

20 Points

- ❏ Create a worksheet for your classmates in which you need to know how to calculate the radius, diameter, and circumference of a circle in order to solve real-world problems.

- ❏ Create a collage of circular objects. Using a ruler, measure the radius and diameter and calculate the circumference for each. Record your measurements beside each object in your collage.

50 Points

- ❏ Create a children's book about circles and the relationships between their properties.

- ❏ Your teacher would like to buy the largest circular rug she can use to cover your classroom floor. They sell them by diameter. Make a poster to propose to your teacher the size of rug she should purchase and include a drawing of the pattern and colors you think would be best.

- ❏ Circles have uses in other content areas. Create a PowerPoint presentation that shows at least five examples of how circles and the measures of their radii (plural of radius) are used in each of the other content areas.

- ❏ Free choice—prepare a proposal form and submit your idea for approval.

80 Points

- ❏ There is a special relationship between the diameter and the circumference of a circle. Design a measuring activity that allows you to figure out this relationship. You should test at least 10 objects to confirm your results.

- ❏ Scientists use circles and triangulation to locate the epicenter of an earthquake. Research this unique use of circles and create a lesson for your classmates that shares your knowledge and helps them solve an epicenter problem you have designed for them.

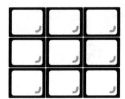

Measuring Shapes

Game Show Menu

Objectives Covered Through This Menu and These Activities

- Students will calculate area, surface area, perimeter, and volume of various geometric shapes.
- Students will identify how changing one dimension can alter an object's perimeter, area, or volume.

Materials Needed by Students for Completion

- Rulers and measuring tape
- Poster board or large white paper
- Coat hangers (for mobile)
- Index cards (for mobile)
- String (for mobile)
- DVD or VHS recorder (for news report)
- Materials for board games (e.g., folders, colored cards)
- Ping pong ball

Special Notes on the Use of This Menu

This menu allows students the opportunity to create a news report. Although students enjoy producing their own videos, there often are difficulties obtaining the equipment and scheduling the use of the video recorder. This can be modified by allowing students to act out the news report (like a play) or, if students have the technology, they may wish to produce a Webcam or Flash version of their news report.

Time Frame

- 2–3 weeks—Students are given the menu as the unit is started and the guidelines and point expectations on the back of the menu are discussed. As lessons are taught throughout the unit, students and the teacher can refer back to the options associated with that topic. The teacher will go over all of the options for the topic being covered and have students place checkmarks in the boxes next to the activities they are most interested in completing. As teaching continues throughout the 2–3 weeks, activities are discussed, chosen, and submitted for grading.

- 1 week—At the beginning of the unit, the teacher chooses an activity from each area he or she feels would be most valuable for students. Stations can be set up in the classroom. These activities are available for student choice throughout the week as regular instruction takes place.
- 1–2 days—The teacher chooses an activity from an objective to use with the entire class during that lesson time.

Suggested Forms

- All-purpose rubric
- Free-choice proposal form for point-based products

Guidelines for the Measuring Shapes Game Show Menu

- You must choose at least one activity from each topic area.

- You may not do more than two activities in any one topic area for credit. (You are, of course, welcome to do more than two for your own investigation.)

- Grading will be ongoing, so turn in products as you complete them.

- All free-choice proposals must be turned in and approved *prior* to working on that free choice.

- You must earn 100 points for a 100%. You may earn extra credit up to _____ points.

- You must show your teacher your plan for completion by: _____.

Measuring Shapes

Perimeter	Area	Surface Area	Volume	Changes in Dimensions	Points for Each Level
❑ Choose four objects or rooms in your school and measure their perimeter. Present the objects or rooms and your data. (15 pts.)	❑ Create a poster that shows how to find the areas of at least three different shapes. (10 pts.)	❑ Create a mobile with different space figures, the formulas for calculating the surface area, and your results from the calculation. (15 pts.)	❑ Create a brochure that shows examples of the different solids and explains how to calculate the volume of each. (10 pts.)	❑ Create a brochure that shares how changing the measure of one side of a figure impacts its perimeter, area, and volume. (15 pts.)	10–15 points
❑ Choose six different locations on your body and measure their perimeter. Use this information to approximate the volume of material within that area of the body. (25 pts.)	❑ Create an advertisement for a product whose area is its main selling point. (25 pts.)	❑ The ancient Greeks tried to calculate the surface area of the Earth. Create a poster that shows how this calculation could be accomplished. (25 pts.)	❑ Design a board game that allows players to estimate the volume of classroom objects and provides an opportunity for them to test their estimates. (25 pts.)	❑ Create a model that shows how volume changes as perimeter changes. (20 pts.)	20–25 points
❑ Your school is thinking of putting a new fence all the way around the outside area including the fields. Determine how to accomplish this task. After measuring, make a proposal for the amount of fencing needed and then complete the calculations. (30 pts.)	❑ You have been given the task of recarpeting your school's library. Develop a plan for how to accomplish this task. After measuring, calculate the amount of carpet needed and a reasonable cost. (30 pts.)	❑ The surface area of a lake affects how quickly the water from the lake evaporates. Investigate this phenomenon and create a news report that explains this phenomena and shares calculations about a lake in your state. (30 pts.)	❑ Your teacher made the comment that more than 100,000 ping pong balls would fit in the school gym. Develop a calculation method to see if he or she is right. After taking some measurements, propose the amount the gym would hold. (30 pts.)	❑ Research at least four geometric monuments around the world. Create a poster with a picture of each and their measurements. Show how the other dimensions will change if you created a scale model no taller than 12 inches. (30 pts.)	30 points
Free Choice (prior approval) (25–50 pts.)	**Free Choice** (prior approval) (25–50 pts.)	**Free Choice** (prior approval) (25–50 pts.)	**Free Choice** (prior approval) (25–50 pts.)	**Free Choice** (prior approval) (25–50 pts.)	25–50 points
Total:	**Total:**	**Total:**	**Total:**	**Total:**	**Total Grade:**

Surface Area

List Menu

Objectives Covered Through This Menu and These Activities

- Students will demonstrate how to calculate the total and lateral surface area of various space figures including spheres, prisms, and cylinders.
- Students will use nets to show how surface area is created.
- Students will understand the relationship between volume and surface area.

Materials Needed by Students for Completion

- Poster board or large white paper
- Large blank lined index cards (for instruction card)
- Microsoft PowerPoint or other slideshow software
- Blank index cards (for concentration card game)
- Graph paper

Time Frame

- 1–2 weeks—Students are given the menu as the unit is started and the guidelines and point expectations are discussed. Students usually will need to earn 100 points for 100%, although there is an opportunity for extra credit if the teacher would like to use another target number. Because this menu covers one topic in depth, the teacher will go over all of the options on the menu and have students place checkmarks in the boxes next to the activities they are most interested in completing. Teachers will need to set aside a few moments to sign the agreement at the bottom of the page with each student. As instruction continues, activities are completed by students and submitted for grading.
- 1–2 days—The teacher chooses an activity or product from an objective to use with the entire class during that lesson time.

Suggested Forms

- All-purpose rubric
- Free-choice proposal form for point-based products

Name:_____ Date:_____

Surface Area

Guidelines:
1. You may complete as many of the activities listed within the time period.
2. You may choose any combination of activities.
3. Your goal is 100 points. You may earn up to _____ points extra credit.
4. You may be as creative as you like within the guidelines listed below.
5. You must show your plan to your teacher by _____.
6. Activities may be turned in at any time during the working time period. They will be graded and recorded on this sheet as you continue to work, so keep it safe!

Plan to Do	Activity to Complete	Point Value	Date Completed	Points Earned
	Your PE teacher has proposed a challenge: Figure out how many dimples are on a basketball. Using your knowledge of scale factor and surface area, create an instruction card that shows your answer and how to calculate it.	25		
	Create a PowerPoint presentation that shows how to calculate the total and lateral surface area of various space figures.	15		
	Use household objects to create an imaginary animal made out of geometric shapes that includes at least one of each of the following: cylinder, prism, cone, and sphere. Calculate its surface area and show your work.	30		
	Write and illustrate a children's book about a prism and its quest to have its total surface area calculated.	30		
	Create a set of concentration cards for matching the formulas for different space figures with a drawing of the figure.	15		
	Using graph paper, create your own set of nets for various geometric shapes and show how you use them to calculate total surface area.	15		
	Design a worksheet that focuses on situations where lateral or total surface area is calculated.	20		
	Investigate other space figures such as icosahedrons or dodecahedrons. Develop a theory about the how to calculate the total surface area of these figures. Create a poster that shows your findings with calculations to prove your thoughts.	30		
	Create Three Facts and a Fib for the surface area of space figures.	20		
	Develop a class lesson that teaches your classmates about the relationship between surface area and the volume of an object.	30		
	Submit your free-choice proposal form for a product of your choice.	15–30		
	Total number of points you are planning to earn.	**Total points earned:**		

I am planning to complete _____ activities that could earn up to a total of _____ points.

Teacher's initials _____ Student's signature _____

Congruence and Similarity

20-50-80 Menu

Objectives Covered Through This Menu and These Activities

- Students will recognize similar and congruent objects.
- Students will state why objects are similar or congruent.

Materials Needed by Students for Completion

- Project cube template
- Magazines (for collage)
- Ruler (for comic strip)
- Microsoft PowerPoint or other slideshow software
- Materials for class lesson

Time Frame

- 1–2 weeks—Students are given the menu as the unit is started, and the teacher discusses all of the product options on the menu. As the different options are discussed, students will choose products that add to a total of 100 points. As the lessons progress through the week(s), the teacher and students refer back to the menu options associated with the content being taught.
- 1–2 days—The teacher chooses an activity or product from the menu to use with the entire class.

Suggested Forms

- All-purpose rubric
- Student-taught lesson rubric
- Free-choice proposal form for point-based projects

Congruence and Similarity

Directions: Choose two activities from the menu below. The activities must total 100 points. Place a checkmark next to each box to show which activities you will complete. All activities must be completed by _____.

---

20 Points

❑ Create a brochure that discusses how to determine if shapes are congruent or similar. Have fun with the graphics you include!

❑ Make a Venn diagram to compare and contrast *congruent* and *similar*.

---

50 Points

❑ Create a collage of different items that also are similar somehow. Include measurements that prove their similarity.

❑ Create a comic strip in which the main characters are created from congruent figures.

❑ Make a cube that has six different similar shapes on its sides. Include your calculations that show that the shapes are all similar.

❑ Free choice—prepare a proposal form and submit your idea for approval.

---

80 Points

❑ There are rules that can be used to prove if two triangles are congruent or similar. Investigate these rules and create a PowerPoint presentation in which you explain the rules, share examples of the rules, and discuss their importance.

❑ Design a class lesson to teach and reinforce how to identify similar and congruent figures. Include instruction that helps your classmates create both congruent and similar figures.

Similar Figures Cube

Make a cube that has six different similar shapes on its sides. Include your calculations that show that the shapes are all similar. Use this pattern or create your own cube.

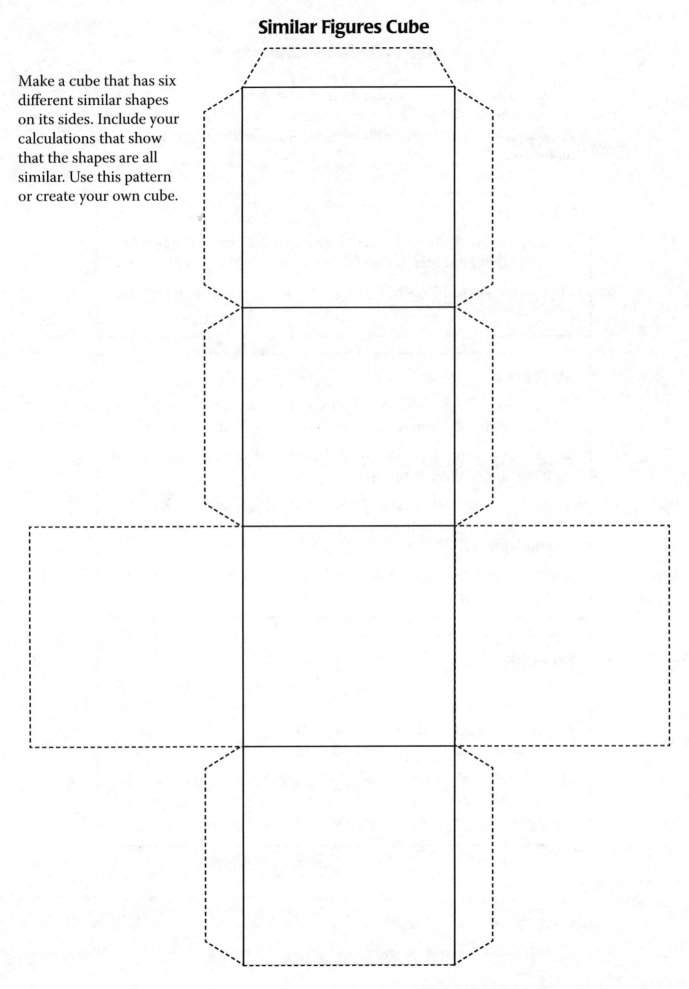

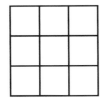

Pythagorean Theorem

Tic-Tac-Toe Menu

Objectives Covered Through This Menu and These Activities

- Students will solve problems using the Pythagorean theorem.
- Students will provide real-world examples of the Pythagorean theorem.
- Students will understand the different ways the Pythagorean theorem can be represented.

Materials Needed by Students for Completion

- Poster board or large white paper
- Microsoft PowerPoint or other slideshow software
- Materials for model
- Internet access (for WebQuest)

Special Notes on the Use of This Menu

This menu allows students to create a WebQuest. There are multiple versions and templates for WebQuests available on the Internet. Teachers may decide whether to specify a certain format or allow students to create one of their own choosing.

Time Frame

- 2–3 weeks—Students are given the menu as the unit is started. As the teacher presents lessons throughout the week, he or she should refer back to the menu options associated with that content. The teacher will go over all of the options for that content and have students place checkmarks in the boxes that represent the activities they are most interested in completing. As teaching continues over the next 2–3 weeks, activities chosen and completed should make a column or row. When students complete this pattern, they have completed one activity from each content area, learning style, or level of Bloom's, depending on the design of the menu.
- 1 week—At the start of the unit, the teacher chooses the three activities he or she feels are most valuable for the students. Stations can be set up in the classroom. These three activities are available for student choice throughout the week as regular instruction takes place.

- 1–2 days—The teacher chooses an activity from the menu to use with the entire class.

Suggested Forms

- All-purpose rubric
- Free-choice proposal form

Name:_____ Date:_____

Pythagorean Theorem

☐ *Make a Poster* There are different ways to represent the Pythagorean theorem. Create a poster to show them.	☐ *Design a PowerPoint Presentation* Consider all of the different real-world applications of the Pythagorean theorem. Create a PowerPoint presentation that showcases these applications with sample calculations for each.	☐ *You be Pythagoras* Come to class as Pythagoras and share your ideas, your theorem, and how you use it! Be sure you to stay true to your time period in your examples.
☐ *Produce a Play* Use your creativity to write and perform a play about a situation that can be solved with calculation using the Pythagorean theorem. Try to avoid a classroom setting—be creative!	☐ **Free Choice: Pythagorean Theorem** (Fill out your proposal form before beginning the free choice!)	☐ *Design a Flipbook* Create five different word problems based on real-world applications of the Pythagorean theorem. Write your problems in a flipbook, placing your answers and how to solve the problems on another piece of paper.
☐ *Make a WebQuest* Investigate a few different Web sites that discuss the history of the Pythagorean theorem and its practical uses. Create a WebQuest that introduces users to both of these.	☐ *Make a Model* Create a model that represents the Pythagorean theorem. Include at least two problems that your model can assist in solving.	☐ *Create Three Facts and a Fib* There are many types of distance problems that can be solved using the Pythagorean theorem. Create Three Facts and a Fib about what types of problems it can or cannot solve.

Check the boxes you plan to complete. They should form a tic-tac-toe across or down.
All products are due by: _____.

Mathematical Proofs

List Menu

Objectives Covered Through This Menu and These Activities

- Students will state why proofs are necessary.
- Students will understand the steps needed to write mathematical proofs.
- Students will state available information that could be used in mathematical proofs.

Materials Needed by Students for Completion

- Blank index cards (for trading cards)
- Project cube template
- DVD or VHS recorder (for educational video)
- Microsoft PowerPoint or other slideshow software
- Poster board or large white paper

Special Notes on the Use of This Menu

This menu allows students to create a WebQuest. There are multiple versions and templates for WebQuests available on the Internet. Teachers may decide whether to specify a certain format or allow students to create one of their own choosing.

This menu gives students the opportunity to create an educational video. Although students enjoy producing their own videos, there often are difficulties obtaining the equipment and scheduling the use of the video recorder. This can be modified by allowing students to act out the educational video (like a play) or, if students have the technology, they may wish to produce a Webcam or Flash version of their video.

Time Frame

- 1–2 weeks—Students are given the menu as the unit is started and the guidelines and point expectations are discussed. Students usually will need to earn 100 points for 100%, although there is an opportunity for extra credit if the teacher would like to use another target number. Because this menu covers one topic in depth, the teacher will go over all of the options on the menu and have students place checkmarks in the boxes next to the activities they are most interested in completing. Teachers will need to set aside a few moments to sign the agreement at the bottom of the page with each student. As instruction continues, activities are completed by students and submitted for grading.

- 1–2 days—The teacher chooses an activity or product from an objective to use with the entire class during that lesson time.

Suggested Forms

- All-purpose rubric
- Student-taught lesson rubric
- Free-choice proposal form for point-based products

Name:_____ Date:_____

Mathematical Proofs

Guidelines:
1. You may complete as many of the activities listed within the time period.
2. You may choose any combination of activities.
3. Your goal is 100 points. You may earn up to _____ points extra credit.
4. You may be as creative as you like within the guidelines listed below.
5. You must show your plan to your teacher by _____.
6. Activities may be turned in at any time during the working time period. They will be graded and recorded on this sheet as you continue to work, so keep it safe!

Plan to Do	Activity to Complete	Point Value	Date Completed	Points Earned
	Create a user-guide brochure that explains how to complete a mathematical proof.	15		
	Create a set of trading cards that include all of the reasons that you can use in your proof.	15		
	Design a cube with six different sets of givens and just one statement to prove. Be sure to provide the answers for your teacher!	30		
	Most students find mathematical proofs difficult. Write a letter to next year's students, giving them at least five hints to make proofs easier. Be as specific as possible.	25		
	Design an educational video in which you discuss why proofs are important, how they help us become better thinkers, and how to solve one.	40		
	Create an advertisement for the benefits of learning how to think logically as is required by proofs.	25		
	The National Council of Teachers of Mathematics believes that mathematical proofs are important for all students. Investigate what they say about them and write a newspaper article sharing their vision.	20		
	Write Three Facts and a Fib for solving proofs.	25		
	Create a PowerPoint presentation that shares the best way to evaluate the reasons used in a mathematical proof.	25		
	Investigate false mathematical proofs (Abbott and Costello is a good place to start). Develop a poster that shows multiple proofs and what makes them false.	20		
	Submit your free-choice proposal form for a product of your choice.	15–30		
	Total number of points you are planning to earn.		**Total points earned:**	

I am planning to complete _____ activities that could earn up to a total of _____ points.

Teacher's initials _____ Student's signature _____

© Prufrock Press Inc. • *Differentiating Instruction With Menus: Middle School Edition: Math*

Mathematical Proofs Cube

Design a cube with six different sets of givens. Record the statement that needs to be proven on the back of the cube. Be sure to provide the answers for your teacher! Use this pattern or create your own cube.

Given:

Given:

Given:

Given:

Given:

Given:

Famous Mathematicians

Tic-Tac-Toe Menu

Objective Covered Through This Menu and These Activities

- Students will identify and investigate famous mathematicians and their contributions.

Materials Needed by Students for Completion

- Scrapbooking materials
- Microsoft PowerPoint or other slideshow software
- Blank index cards (for trading cards)
- DVD or VHS recorder (for news report)

Special Notes on the Use of This Menu

This menu allows students the opportunity to create a news report. Although students enjoy producing their own videos, there often are difficulties obtaining the equipment and scheduling the use of the video recorder. This can be modified by allowing students to act out the news report (like a play) or, if students have the technology, they may wish to produce a Webcam or Flash version of their news report.

Time Frame

- 2–3 weeks—Students are given the menu as the unit is started. As the teacher presents lessons throughout the week, he or she should refer back to the menu options associated with that content. The teacher will go over all of the options for that content and have students place checkmarks in the boxes that represent the activities they are most interested in completing. As teaching continues over the next 2–3 weeks, activities chosen and completed should make a column or row. When students complete this pattern, they have completed one activity from each content area, learning style, or level of Bloom's, depending on the design of the menu.
- 1 week—At the start of the unit, the teacher chooses the three activities he or she feels are most valuable for the students. Stations can be set up in the classroom. These three activities are available for student choice throughout the week as regular instruction takes place.
- 1–2 days—The teacher chooses an activity from the menu to use with the entire class.

Suggested Forms

- All-purpose rubric
- Student-taught lesson rubric
- Free-choice proposal form

Famous Mathematicians

☐ *Design a Windowpane* Create a windowpane for six mathematicians that are important to our current unit of study. Record the mathematicians' names and three facts about them in each windowpane.	☐ *Create a Scrapbook* Choose one mathematician you feel has had the largest impact on the study of mathematics. Create a scrapbook about this mathematician's accomplishments and his or her impact on the world.	☐ *You Be the Star!* Research a famous mathematician and prepare a "You Be the Person" presentation to share with your class.
☐ *Create a PowerPoint Presentation* Choose one significant mathematician from our current unit of study. Create a PowerPoint presentation to accompany a speech on your chosen mathematician and his or her contributions to the study of mathematics.	☐ **Free Choice: Famous Mathematicians** (Fill out your proposal form before beginning the free choice!)	☐ *Write a Newspaper Article* You have been asked to interview a famous mathematician from our current unit of study. Develop appropriate interview questions and write a newspaper article with the information about the mathematician and his or her discoveries.
☐ *Perform a News Report* A mathematician from our current unit of study is being nominated for the "Mathematicians Hall of Fame." Prepare a news report on the mathematician and why he or she is qualifying for this special honor.	☐ *Design a Book Cover* There is a new biography being written about a well-known mathematician of your choice. Design a book cover for this mathematician's biography.	☐ *Create Trading Cards* Create a set of trading cards for at least six mathematicians who made significant contributions to the study of mathematics.

Check the boxes you plan to complete. They should form a tic-tac-toe across or down. All products are due by: _____.

Name:_____ Date:_____

Famous Mathematicians

Archimedes	Benjamin Banneker	Charles Babbage
Georg Cantor	Countess of Lovelace (Augusta Ada King)	René Descartes
Paul Erdös	Euclid	Eukleides
Leonhard Euler	Pierre de Fermat	Fibonacci
Johann Carl Friedrich Gauss	Sophie Germain	Thomas Hobbes
Herman Hollerith	Hypatia of Alexandria	John Kemeny
Blaise Pascal	Plato	Pythagoras
Julia Robinson	Babylonian Impacts on Number System	Zeno of Elea

Euclid

CHAPTER 7

Graphing and Measurement

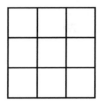

Graphing

Tic-Tac-Toe Menu

Objectives Covered Through This Menu and These Activities
- Students will evaluate which graph is best for showing certain types of data.
- Students will choose appropriate graphs to show their own data.
- Students will be able to create circle graphs, bar graphs, and histograms.

Materials Needed by Students for Completion
- Materials for board games (e.g., folders, colored cards)
- Microsoft PowerPoint or other slideshow software
- Scrapbooking materials
- Large lined index cards (for recipe card)
- DVD or VHS recorder (for news report)
- Coat hangers (for mobile)
- Index cards (for mobile)
- String (for mobile)

Special Notes on the Use of This Menu

This menu gives students the opportunity to create a news report. Although students enjoy producing their own videos, there often are difficulties obtaining the equipment and scheduling the use of the video recorder. This can be modified by allowing students to act out their news report (like a play) or, if students have the technology, they may wish to produce a Webcam or Flash version of their news report.

Time Frame
- 2–3 weeks—Students are given the menu as the unit is started. As the teacher presents lessons throughout the week, he or she should refer back to the menu options associated with that content. The teacher will go over all of the options for that content and have students place checkmarks in the boxes that represent the activities they are most interested in completing. As teaching continues over the next 2–3 weeks, activities chosen and completed should make a column or row. When students complete this pattern, they have completed one activity

from each content area, learning style, or level of Bloom's, depending on the design of the menu.

- 1 week—At the start of the unit, the teacher chooses the three activities he or she feels are most valuable for the students. Stations can be set up in the classroom. These three activities are available for student choice throughout the week as regular instruction takes place.
- 1–2 days—The teacher chooses an activity from the menu to use with the entire class.

Suggested Forms

- All-purpose rubric
- Free-choice proposal form

Graphing

☐ *Make Your Own Graph* Create a survey that will provide data that could be shown on a circle graph. Have at least five people complete your survey and create your graph.	☐ *Which Graph Is Best?* Make a PowerPoint presentation that shows how to choose a graph based on the information you would like to present.	☐ *Same Data, Different Graph?* Create a board game in which players analyze data presented on different types of graphs.
☐ *Same Data, Different Graph?* Create a scrapbook of different examples of bias in how data are presented on different graphs to make the data appear in a certain way.	☐ **Free Choice: Make Your Own Graph** (Fill out your proposal form before beginning the free choice!)	☐ *Which Graph Is Best?* Design a lesson for your classmates to help them figure out when to use each type of graph: circle, bar, line, and histograms.
☐ *Which Graph Is Best?* Build a mobile for graphing with at least four different types of graphs, examples of each one, and the best use for that graph.	☐ *Same Data, Different Graph?* Create a news report in which the reporter seems to have two very different pieces of information but is, in fact, really two different graphs of the same information.	☐ *Make Your Own Graph* Create a recipe card for making a histogram. Design a survey and use your card to create your own histogram. Include a real-world example of data you have gathered.

Check the boxes you plan to complete. They should form a tic-tac-toe across or down.

All products are due by: _____.

Coordinate Planes

Tic-Tac-Toe Menu

Objectives Covered Through This Menu and These Activities

- Students will generate mathematically similar shapes by enlarging and reducing through dilation.
- Students will recognize translations and reflections in art and architecture.
- Students will locate and name points on a coordinate plane.

Materials Needed by Students for Completion

- Information on M. C. Escher
- Graph paper
- Materials for bulletin board display
- Poster board or large white paper
- Large lined index cards (for instruction card)
- Scrapbooking materials

Special Notes on the Use of This Menu

This menu allows students to create a bulletin board display. Some classrooms may only have one bulletin board, so the teacher can divide the board into sections, or additional classroom wall or hall space can be sectioned off for the creation of these displays. Students can plan their display based on the amount of space they are assigned.

Time Frame

- 2–3 weeks—Students are given the menu as the unit is started. As the teacher presents lessons throughout the week, he or she should refer back to the menu options associated with that content. The teacher will go over all of the options for that content and have students place checkmarks in the boxes that represent the activities they are most interested in completing. As teaching continues over the next 2–3 weeks, activities chosen and completed should make a column or row. When students complete this pattern, they have completed one activity from each content area, learning style, or level of Bloom's, depending on the design of the menu.
- 1 week—At the start of the unit, the teacher chooses the three activities he or she feels are most valuable for the students. Stations can be

set up in the classroom. These three activities are available for student choice throughout the week as regular instruction takes place.

- 1–2 days—The teacher chooses an activity from the menu to use with the entire class.

Suggested Forms

- All-purpose rubric
- Free-choice proposal form

Coordinate Planes

☐ *Ordered Pairs* Your classmates feel they know all about ordered pairs. Create a worksheet for your classmates that will challenge them by practicing plotting and finding points on a coordinate plane.	☐ *Translations and Reflections* The artist M. C. Escher created some of his artwork using translations and tessellations of a symmetrical object. Research these works and after choosing a symmetrical object that represents your personality, create your own masterpiece. Include a brief statement about how you used translations.	☐ *Dilations* Create a class lesson in which you teach your classmates how to draw dilations on a coordinate graph, as well as how to determine the scale factor of the dilations using the ordered pairs.
☐ *Dilations* Dilations can be used to enlarge or reduce shapes on a coordinate plane. They also can be used to enlarge or reduce drawings by placing a reference grid over a drawing. Investigate this process and after choosing a drawing, enlarge or reduce it at least twice.	☐ **Free Choice: Ordered Pairs** (Fill out your proposal form before beginning the free choice!)	☐ *Translations and Reflections* Do reflections always have a line of symmetry? Create a bulletin board display that answers this question by sharing various examples.
☐ *Translations and Reflections* Architects often use translations and reflections of geometric shapes when they design their buildings. Create a scrapbook of local photographs or pictures from magazines that show this technique. Label the translations and reflections.	☐ *Dilations* Create an instruction card that explains how to complete reductions and enlargements. Include an example of each on the back of your card.	☐ *Ordered Pairs* Using a piece of graph paper, make a drawing or picture. Write instructions directing other students to create your drawing using only the coordinates in the correct order.

Check the boxes you plan to complete. They should form a tic-tac-toe across or down.

All products are due by: _____.

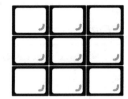

Transformations and Symmetry

Game Show Menu

Objectives Covered Through This Menu and These Activities

- Students will identify an object's line and rotational symmetry.
- Students will explain whether each transformation creates a congruent or similar image.
- Students will recognize translations and reflections in art and architecture.
- Students will generate mathematically similar shapes by enlarging and reducing through dilation.

Materials Needed by Students for Completion

- Scrapbooking materials
- Graph paper
- Microsoft PowerPoint or other slideshow software
- Internet access (for WebQuest)
- Large blank lined index cards (for instruction card)
- Materials for a class game

Special Notes on the Use of This Menu

Students are given the opportunity to create a game for the class. The length of the game is not stated in the product guidelines, so the teacher can determine what works best. It may be good to have students start with shorter games and work up to longer games with a review focus.

This menu allows students to create a WebQuest. There are multiple versions and templates for WebQuests available on the Internet. Teachers may decide whether to specify a certain format or allow students to create one of their own choosing.

Time Frame

- 2–3 weeks—Students are given the menu as the unit is started and the guidelines and point expectations on the back of the menu are discussed. As lessons are taught throughout the unit, students and the teacher can refer back to the options associated with that topic. The teacher will go over all of the options for the topic being covered and have students place checkmarks in the boxes next to the activities they are most interested in completing. As teaching continues throughout the 2–3 weeks, activities are discussed, chosen, and submitted for grading.

- 1 week—At the beginning of the unit, the teacher chooses an activity from each area that he or she feels would be most valuable for students. Stations can be set up in the classroom. These activities are available for student choice throughout the week as regular instruction takes place.
- 1–2 days—The teacher chooses an activity from an objective to use with the entire class during that lesson time.

Suggested Forms

- All-purpose rubric
- Student-taught lesson rubric
- Free-choice proposal form for point-based products

Guidelines for the Transformations and Symmetry Game Show Menu

- You must choose at least one activity from each topic area.

- You may not do more than two activities in any one topic area for credit. (You are, of course, welcome to do more than two for your own investigation.)

- Grading will be ongoing, so turn in products as you complete them.

- All free-choice proposals must be turned in and approved *prior* to working on that free choice.

- You must earn 100 points for a 100%. You may earn extra credit up to _____ points.

- You must show your teacher your plan for completion by:_____.

Transformations and Symmetry

Symmetry	Translations	Rotations	Dilations	Points for Each Level
☐ Create a scrapbook with at least 10 different real-world examples of line and rotational symmetry. Label each with its type of symmetry, as well the line or point of rotation. (15 pts.)	☐ Create a folded quiz book about the different types of translations and how to draw them. (10 pts.)	☐ Create an instruction card that explains how to complete a rotation. Include an example of each step on the back of your card, as well as how rotations depend on symmetry. (15 pts.)	☐ Create a worksheet that will give your classmates the opportunity to practice creating dilations and identifying their scale factor. (15 pts.)	10–15 points
☐ Most organisms in nature have either lateral (line) or radial (rotational) symmetry. After investigating these organisms, use graph paper to assist you in creating a human with rotational symmetry. (25 pts.)	☐ Choose at least two artists who use translations in their artwork. Create a PowerPoint presentation about their art and the importance of translations in their creations. (25 pts.)	☐ There are many interactive Web sites that use games and simulations to teach rotations. Create a WebQuest that focuses on how to create and determine the symmetry of a rotation. (25 pts.)	☐ Dilations can be used to enlarge or reduce shapes using a coordinate plane. They also can be used to enlarge or reduce drawings by placing the coordinate plane over a drawing. Investigate this process and after choosing a drawing, enlarge or reduce it at least twice. (25 pts.)	20–25 points
☐ Create a children's book about symmetry in the world around us. Be imaginative in the examples you choose and their explanations. (30 pts.)	☐ Tessellations often are used when designing buildings. Research this technique and after choosing a symmetrical object that represents your personality, create a tessellation of your own that is at least 24 cm in length. Include a brief statement about how your artwork depends on translation. (30 pts.)	☐ Create a lesson for your classmates that allows them all to be actively involved in practicing how to create rotations. (30 pts.)	☐ Create a class game that asks teams to practice their dilation drawing skills. (30 pts.)	30 points
Free Choice (prior approval) (25–50 pts.)	**Free Choice** (prior approval) (25–50 pts.)	**Free Choice** (prior approval) (25–50 pts.)	**Free Choice** (prior approval) (25–50 pts.)	25–50 points
Total:	**Total:**	**Total:**	**Total:**	**Total Grade:**

Measurement

Baseball Menu

Objectives Covered Through This Menu and These Activities

- Students will estimate length, capacity, weight, and temperature in standard and metric units.
- Students will solve problems using length, capacity, weight, and temperature in standard and metric units.
- Students will solve real-world problems using time and schedules.

Materials Needed by Students for Completion

- Coat hangers (for mobile)
- Blank index cards (for mobile and concentration cards)
- String (for mobile)
- Newspapers
- Microsoft PowerPoint or other slideshow software
- Internet access (for research and scheduling)
- Graduated cylinders, measuring cups
- Triple beam balance, spring scale
- Thermometers
- Graph paper
- Scrapbooking materials

Time Frame

- 2–3 weeks—Students are given the menu as the unit is started and the guidelines and point expectations on the top of the menu are discussed. Usually, students are expected to complete 100 points. Because this menu covers one topic in depth, the teacher will go over all of the options for the topic being covered and have students place checkmarks in the boxes next to the activities they are most interested in completing. As instruction continues, activities are completed by students and submitted for grading.
- 1 week—At the beginning of the unit, the teacher chooses 1–2 higher level activities that can be integrated into whole-group instruction throughout the week.
- 1–2 days—The teacher chooses an activity from an objective to use with the entire class during that lesson time.

Suggested Forms

- All-purpose rubric
- Free-choice proposal form for point-based projects

Measurement

Look through the following choices and decide how you want to make your game add to 100 points. Singles are worth 10, doubles are worth 30, triples are worth 50, and home runs are worth 100. Choose any combination you want. Place a checkmark next to each choice you are going to complete. Make sure that your points equal 100!

Singles—10 Points Each

❏ Create a mobile with the different units for measuring length, weight, capacity, and temperature, as well as an example of an object that would be best measured with each unit.

❏ Go through the newspaper to locate articles that give examples of length, weight, and capacity. Prepare a poster with at least 10 examples.

❏ Certain household items have temperature restrictions for their use. Research why they have these restrictions and find eight examples of these items in your home. Prepare a poster that shows the items and how temperature affects them.

❏ Create a capacity and length collection. Collect two nontoxic household items that are measured in each of the following units: centimeters, inches, meters, cups, pints, quarts, and gallons. This will give you a total of 14 items to bring to class.

❏ Create an acrostic for capacity, length, and weight. Be sure to use units in your phrases!

❏ Create a set of concentration cards that would allow players to match units with their measurements.

Doubles—30 Points Each

❏ Create a "guess the measure" game. In this game, players will need to estimate and measure the length and weight of target items. Be creative in the design of the game.

❏ There are many time zones around the world. Prepare a PowerPoint presentation that describes the reason for time zones and the reasons why the zones are not always straight lines.

❏ A movie theater is holding a day-long movie marathon for just $10. Analyze the movie times of current films and create a schedule that allows you to see as many movies as possible within the day. You cannot leave one movie for another and you cannot see the same movie twice!

❏ All household items that hold liquids need to be marked in both metric and standard units. Develop a system to test the accuracy of these recorded measurements. Test four household items and present your data in a table.

❏ Create a map of your room. (You may have to do some measuring!) Develop a scale for your map using appropriate units.

❏ Design new units for measuring length, capacity, and weight. Create a brochure that explains the new units, how they are measured, and the equivalents to our current units.

Triples—50 Points Each

❏ Design an experiment in which your classmates would practice estimating and measuring in milliliters and liters.

❏ Develop a strategy that would help you accurately guess an object's weight in grams and ounces, as well as its length in inches and centimeters. Record your method and all of your trials, and be ready to show your skill to your classmates.

❏ Weight often is used in packaging, rather than counting items. How accurate is this method? Choose a product that is packaged based on weight in grams rather than a count of the items and devise a way to confirm the accuracy of this method.

❏ Create the perfect schedule for a week. It should be designed for people your age and all the interests they have. Note: You must go to school and you must sleep!

Home Run—100 Points

❏ You are participating in a challenge to race around the world. Prepare a scrapbook that details your itinerary, your suitcase choice, and a list of what you will bring with you on the trip—be specific because weight matters! You must meet all of the criteria of the competition. The competition states:

- You must visit at least seven major airports and six continents.

- You must get at least 8 hours of sleep every 24 hours, although you can sleep on a plane if the flight is longer than 8 hours. Otherwise, you must stay in a location 8 hours for sleep. Be sure you do not cut your flight too close, as taxis are not always reliable!

- You must bring enough clothing to be able to change at least once every 24 hours, but cannot exceed the 14-pound carry-on luggage limit used by some overseas airlines. You may need to weigh your clothing to be sure it does not exceed the limit.

- Your suitcase must not be larger than a total of 45 linear inches (length added to height added to width), so choose wisely.

- You need to keep in mind the restrictions on liquids on airlines. Investigate these restrictions and plan accordingly with the items you need to pack for your daily hygiene needs.

I Chose:

_____ Singles (10 points each)

_____ Doubles (30 points each)

_____ Triples (50 points each)

_____ Home Run (100 points)

CHAPTER 8

Basic Algebra

Using Variables

20-50-80 Menu

Objectives Covered Through This Menu and These Activities

- Students will understand the purpose of a variable in a mathematical statement.
- Students will recognize the common variables used in formulas.

Materials Needed by Students for Completion

- Blank index cards (for trading cards)
- Project cube template
- Materials for board games (e.g., folders, colored cards)
- Poster board or large white paper

Time Frame

- 1–2 weeks—Students are given the menu as the unit is started, and the teacher discusses all of the product options on the menu. As the different options are discussed, students will choose products that add to a total of 100 points. As the lessons progress through the week(s), the teacher and students refer back to the menu options associated with the content being taught.
- 1–2 days—The teacher chooses an activity or product from the menu to use with the entire class.

Suggested Forms

- All-purpose rubric
- Free-choice proposal form for point-based projects

Using Variables

Directions: Choose two activities from the menu below. The activities must total 100 points. Place a checkmark next to each box to show which activities you will complete. All activities must be completed by _____.

---

20 Points

❑ Make a set of trading cards for all of the variables you have used in formulas for the last 2 years. For each variable, include the formulas it impacts. Remember that a variable may be in more than one formula!

❑ Create a variable cube to help others become more familiar with the use of certain variables in equations. Users will roll the cube and name all of the formulas they can with that variable in it. Place common variables on each side and include an answer sheet with all of the formulas that include each variable on the cube.

---

50 Points

❑ When looking at formulas and variables, you will notice some variables are written as capital letters, while others are lowercase. Investigate the reason behind this difference in notation. Create a brochure that explains the format of a formula. Be sure to include specific examples to support your information.

❑ Create Three Facts and a Fib about how variables can be used in an equation or formula.

❑ Create a board game on variables that focuses on what they are and how they are used.

❑ Free choice—prepare a proposal form and submit your idea for approval.

---

80 Points

❑ The job of a variable is to stand in for a value. It probably would be very frustrating not having an identity of your own. Write and perform a play about the job of a particular variable and the numbers he has replaced recently.

❑ Using variables in a mathematical statement can be confusing to students. Create a children's book that explains how and why they are used. Make the use of variables fun and easy to understand.

Using Variables Cube

Place common variables from formulas you use frequently on each side of the cube so users can roll the cube and practice naming the variable that appears. Use this pattern or create your own cube.

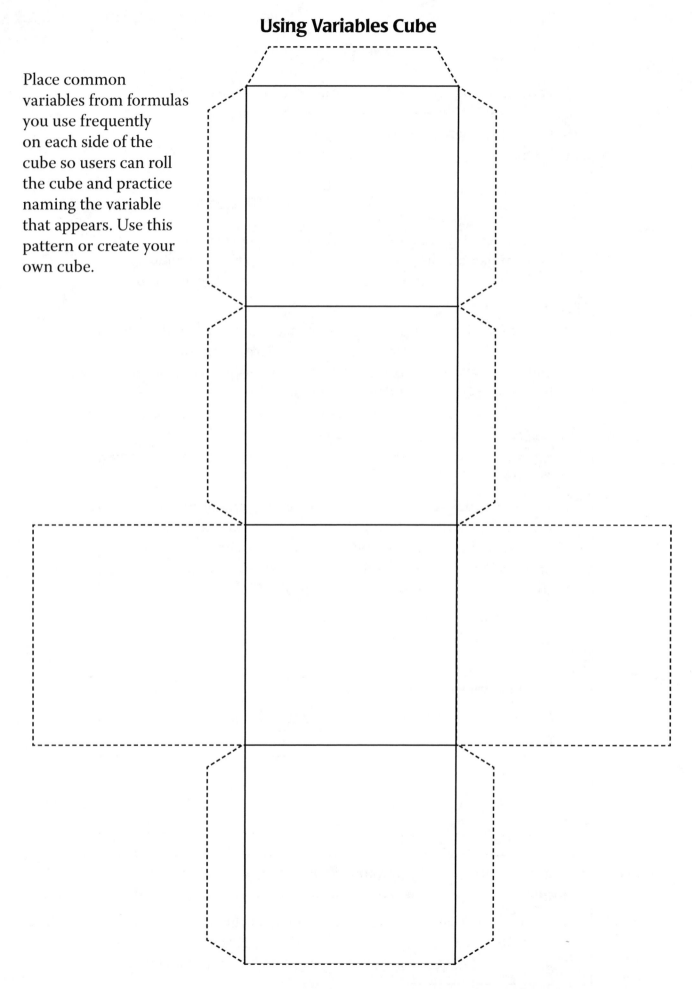

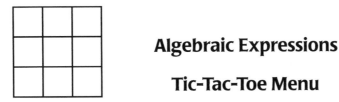

Algebraic Expressions

Tic-Tac-Toe Menu

Objectives Covered Through This Menu and These Activities

- Students will match algebraic expressions with their verbal statement.
- Students will translate verbal phrases into algebraic expressions.
- Students will brainstorm the situations created through algebraic expressions.

Materials Needed by Students for Completion

- Blank index cards (for concentration cards)
- DVD or VHS recorder (for news report and commercial)
- Materials for bulletin board display
- Newspapers

Special Notes on the Use of This Menu

This menu allows students to create a bulletin board display. Some classrooms may only have one bulletin board, so the teacher can divide the board into sections, or additional classroom wall or hall space can be sectioned off for the creation of these displays. Students can plan their display based on the amount of space they are assigned.

This menu also gives students the opportunity to create a news report or commercial. Although students enjoy producing their own videos, there often are difficulties obtaining the equipment and scheduling the use of the video recorder. This can be modified by allowing students to act out the news report or commercial (like a play) or, if students have the technology, they may wish to produce a Webcam or Flash version of their news report.

Time Frame

- 2–3 weeks—Students are given the menu as the unit is started. As the teacher presents lessons throughout the week, he or she should refer back to the menu options associated with that content. The teacher will go over all of the options for that content and have students place checkmarks in the boxes that represent the activities they are most interested in completing. As teaching continues over the next 2–3 weeks, activities chosen and completed should make a column or row. When students complete this pattern, they have completed one activity from each content area, learning style, or level of Bloom's, depending on the design of the menu.

- 1 week—At the start of the unit, the teacher chooses the three activities he or she feels are most valuable for the students. Stations can be set up in the classroom. These three activities are available for student choice throughout the week as regular instruction takes place.
- 1–2 days—The teacher chooses an activity from the menu to use with the entire class.

Suggested Forms

- All-purpose rubric
- Free-choice proposal form

Name:_____ Date:_____

Algebraic Expressions

☐ *Create Concentration Cards* Brainstorm a list of situations and the algebraic expressions that might represent them. Create a set of concentration cards that allows users to match them. Be sure and include addition, subtraction, multiplication, and division in your situations.	☐ *Contemplate a Commercial* Create a commercial about a special bargain available to customers of a new store that just opened. The bargain is represented by: $164 - 3(x + 2)$.	☐ *Build a Bulletin Board* Look through newspapers and magazines and collect examples of situations that could be expressed algebraically. Create a bulletin board display for your examples and the algebraic expressions that accompanies them.
☐ *Think Through Three Facts and a Fib* Choose a situation that could be represented algebraically. Create Three Facts and a Fib about the expression created from the situation.	☐ *Free Choice: Algebraic Expressions* (Fill out your proposal form before beginning the free choice!)	☐ *Perform a Play* Consider the following algebraic expression: $2(x + 4) - 3$. Create a play that shows the situation behind this expression. Be expressive and creative in your story development.
☐ *Notify the News* Create a local news report that explains what is happening in the following algebraic expression: $856 + 4(x + 15)$.	☐ *Write a Worksheet* Create a worksheet that allows students to write algebraic expressions to match the situations you have provided.	☐ *Fold a Quaint Quiz Book* Brainstorm at least 10 different situations that can be expressed through algebraic expressions. Use these situations to create a folded quiz book.

Check the boxes you plan to complete. They should form a tic-tac-toe across or down.
All products are due by: _____.

Independent and Dependent Statements

List Menu

Objectives Covered Through This Menu and These Activities

- Students will identify the dependent and independent statements in everyday situations.
- Students will apply dependent and independent statements to numerical sentences.

Materials Needed by Students for Completion

- One copy of *Fortunately* by Remy Charlip
- Materials for board games (e.g., folders, colored cards)
- Magazines (for collage)
- Blank index cards (for concentration cards)
- Materials for bulletin board display
- Poster board or large white paper
- Project cube template

Special Notes on the Use of This Menu

This menu allows students to create a bulletin board display. Some classrooms may only have one bulletin board, so either the board can be divided or additional classroom wall or hall space can be sectioned off for the creation of these displays. Students can plan their display based on the amount of space they are assigned.

Time Frame

- 1–2 weeks—Students are given the menu as the unit is started and the guidelines and point expectations are discussed. Students usually will need to earn 100 points for 100%, although there is an opportunity for extra credit if the teacher would like to use another target number. Because this menu covers one topic in depth, the teacher will go over all of the options on the menu and have students place checkmarks in the boxes next to the activities they are most interested in completing. Teachers will need to set aside a few moments to sign the agreement at the bottom of the page with each student. As instruction continues, activities are completed by students and submitted for grading.

- 1–2 days—The teacher chooses an activity or product from an objective to use with the entire class during lesson time.

Suggested Forms

- All-purpose rubric
- Free-choice proposal form for point-based products

Name:_____ Date:_____

Independent and Dependent Statements

Guidelines:

1. You may complete as many of the activities listed within the time period.
2. You may choose any combination of activities.
3. Your goal is 100 points. You may earn up to _____ points extra credit.
4. You may be as creative as you like within the guidelines listed below.
5. You must show your plan to your teacher by _____.
6. Activities may be turned in at any time during the working time period. They will be graded and recorded on this sheet as you continue to work, so keep it safe!

Plan to Do	Activity to Complete	Point Value	Date Completed	Points Earned
	Design a board game to practice dependent and independent events.	20		
	Create a collage of independent and dependent events and label each.	15		
	Create two cubes, one with dependent statements and one with independent statements, that can be used to develop some creative word problems. Use the cubes to write and solve two of your own problems.	30		
	Read the book *Fortunately* by Remy Charlip, which is full of dependent and independent statements. Create your own version of this story. Include a list of the independent and dependent statements found in your book.	30		
	Create a set of independent/dependent concentration cards.	15		
	Design an interactive bulletin board display that provides questions that can be used to determine whether a statement is dependent or independent.	25		
	Create a folded quiz book that gives either a dependent or independent statement and asks users to provide the other part of its statement. Make your statements open-ended enough to allow multiple answers.	20		
	Design a worksheet with at least five real-world word problems that reinforce problem-solving strategies and ask students to identify the independent and dependent statements in the word problems.	25		
	Create a play about a dependent variable who is tired of always be the effect and wants to become independent.	30		
	Submit your free-choice proposal form for a product of your choice.	15–30		
	Total number of points you are planning to earn.	**Total points earned:**		

I am planning to complete _____ activities that could earn up to a total of _____ points.

Teacher's initials _____ Student's signature _____

Independent and Dependent Statements Cube

Create two cubes, one with dependent statements and one with independent statements, that can be used to develop some creative word problems. Use this pattern or create your own cube.

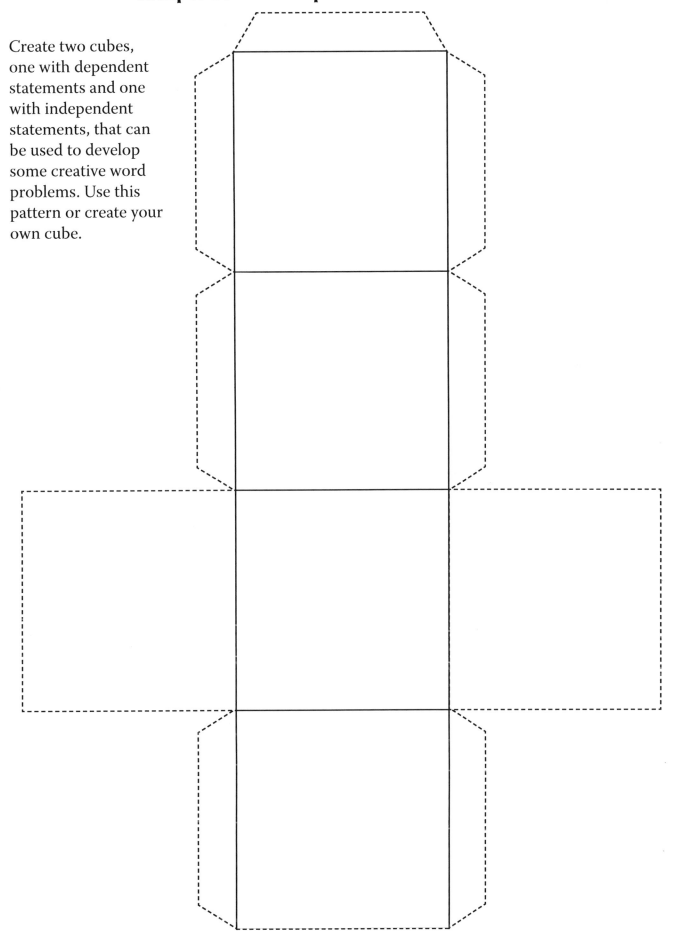

Lines

20-50-80 Menu

Objectives Covered Through This Menu and These Activities

- Students will calculate the slope of a line.
- Students will determine the equation of a line given the line.
- Students will draw a line given a slope and y-intercept.

Materials Needed by Students for Completion

- Large blank index cards (for instruction card)
- Aluminum foil (for quiz board)
- Wires (for quiz board)
- Scrapbooking materials
- Project cube templates
- Socks (for puppets)
- Paper bags (for puppets)

Time Frame

- 1–2 weeks—Students are given the menu as the unit is started, and the teacher discusses all of the product options on the menu. As the different options are discussed, students will choose products that add to a total of 100 points. As the lessons progress through the week(s), the teacher and students refer back to the menu options associated with the content being taught.
- 1–2 days—The teacher chooses an activity or product from the menu to use with the entire class.

Suggested Forms

- All-purpose rubric
- Free-choice proposal form for point-based projects

Lines

Directions: Choose two activities from the menu below. The activities must total 100 points. Place a checkmark next to each box to show which activities you will complete. All activities must be completed by _____.

---

20 Points

❏ Write an instruction card for determining the slope of a line, as well as how to draw a line given the slope and y-intercept. Be sure to include an example of each.

❏ Create a quiz board that allows players to match line equations with their graphs. Don't be too obvious!

---

50 Points

❏ Create a scrapbook of five different pictures that have a line in them. Darken each line and, using a coordinate graph to help, calculate the equation of each line.

❏ Everyone can use a little practice in recognizing different types of slopes and determining the equation of a line. Create a two-cube product that has participants drawing lines by rolling one cube to obtain the slope (include positives and negative, as well as fractional slopes) and the other cube to determine the y-intercept. Use different options for your slopes and include an answer key for all of the options.

❏ The equation of a line is very meaningful, as it can tell a relationship between two variables. Create a meaningful equation and an appropriate puppet that can be used to tell the story behind the equation.

❏ Free choice—prepare a proposal form and submit your idea for approval.

---

80 Points

❏ Lasers and lines often are used in crime lab situations to confirm bullet trajectories. Write and perform a play in which lines and their slopes play an important role. Be sure that the characters have to do some calculations before the conclusion of the play!

❏ Write a children's book that teaches its readers about lines, slope, and y-intercepts using hidden lines.

Lines Cube

Create two cubes: a cube of slopes (using positive, negative, and fractional slopes) and a cube with possible y-intersects. Remember users have to graph it, so be realistic in your numbers! Use this pattern or create two of your own cubes.

Resources

Assouline, S., & Lupkowski-Shoplik, A. (2005). *Developing math talent: A guide for educating gifted and advanced learners in math.* Waco, TX: Prufrock Press.

Bollow, N., Berg, R., & Tyler, M. (2001). *Alien math.* Waco, TX: Prufrock Press.

Charlip, R. (1993). *Fortunately.* New York: Aladdin.

Conway, J. H., & Guy, R. K. (1996). *The book of numbers.* New York: Copernicus.

Fadiman, C. (1962). *The mathematical magpie.* New York: Simon and Schuster.

Field, A. (2006). *The great math experience: Engaging problems for middle school mathematics.* Victoria, BC: Trafford.

Keen, D. (2001). *Talent in the new millennium: Report on year one of the programme.* Retrieved August 29, 2008, from http://www.aare.edu.au/01pap/kee01007.htm

Kleiman, A., & Washington, D. (with Washington, M. F.). (1996). *It's alive! Math like you've never known it before . . . and like you may never know it again.* Waco, TX: Prufrock Press.

Kleiman, A., & Washington, D. (with Washington, M. F.). (1996). *It's alive and kicking: math the way it ought to be—tough, fun, and a little weird.* Waco, TX: Prufrock Press.

Lee, M., & Miller, M. (1997). *Real-life math investigations.* New York: Scholastic.

Lee, M., & Miller, M. (2001). *40 fabulous math mysteries kids can't resist (grades 4–8).* New York: Scholastic.

Miller, M., & Lee, M. (1998). *Problem solving and logic: Great skill-building activities, games, and reproducibles.* New York: Scholastic.

Pappas, T. (1989). *The joy of mathematics: Discovering mathematics all around you.* San Carlos, CA: Wide World Publishing.

Pappas, T. (1993). *Fractals, googols and other mathematical tales.* San Carlos, CA: Wide World Publishing.

Pappas, T. (1997). *Mathematical scandals.* San Carlos, CA: Wide World Publishing.

Schwartz, D. M. (1998). *G is for googol: A math alphabet book.* Berkeley, CA: Tricycle Press.

Scieszka, J., & Smith, L. (1995). *Math curse.* New York: Viking Books.

Tyler, M. W. (1995). *Real life math mysteries.* Waco, TX: Prufrock Press.

Zaccaro, E. (2003). *Primary grade challenge math.* Bellevue, IA: Hickory Grove Press.

Zaccaro, E. (2003). *The 10 things all future mathematicians and scientists must know (but are rarely taught).* Bellevue, IA: Hickory Grove Press.

Zaccaro, E. (2005). *Challenge math for the elementary and middle school student* (2nd ed.). Bellevue, IA: Hickory Grove Press.

Zaccaro, E. (2006). *Becoming a problem solving genius.* Bellevue, IA: Hickory Grove Press.

References

Anderson, L. (Ed.), Krathwohl, D. (Ed.), Airasian, P., Cruikshank, K., Mayer, R., Pintrich, P., et al. (2001). *A taxonomy for learning, teaching, and assessing: A revision of Bloom's taxonomy of educational objectives* (Complete ed.). New York: Longman.

Keen, D. (2001). *Talent in the new millennium: Report on year one of the programme.* Retrieved August 29, 2008, from http://www.aare.edu.au/01pap/kee01007.htm

About the Author

After teaching science for more than 15 years, both overseas and in the U.S., Laurie E. Westphal now works as an independent gifted education and science consultant. She enjoys developing and presenting staff development on differentiation for various districts and conferences, working with teachers to assist them in planning and developing lessons to meet the needs of their advanced students.

Laurie currently resides in Houston, TX, and has made it her goal to share her vision for real-world, product-based lessons that help all students become critical thinkers and effective problem solvers. She is the author of the *Differentiating Instruction With Menus* series as well as *Hands-On Physical Science* and *Science Dictionary for Kids*.